Banchan

Caroline Choe

Photography by
Ghazalle Badiozamani

CHRONICLE BOOKS

SAN FRANCISCO

Banchan

60 Korean American Recipes for Delicious, Shareable Sides

Library of Congress Cataloging-in-Publication Data

Names: Choe, Caroline, author. | Badiozamani, Ghazal, photography.
Title: Banchan : 60 korean american recipes for delicious, shareable
sides / Caroline Choe ; photography by Ghazalle Badiozamani.
Description: San Francisco : Chronicle Books, [2024] | Includes index.
Identifiers: LCCN 2024008879 | ISBN 9781797227115 (hardcover)
Subjects: LCSH: Cooking, Korean. | LCGFT: Cookbooks.
Classification: LCC TX724.5.K65 C455 2024 |
DDC 641.59519--dc23/eng/20240228
LC record available at https://lccn.loc.gov/2024008879

Manufactured in China.

MIX
Paper | Supporting
responsible forestry
FSC™ C008047
FSC
www.fsc.org

Design by RACHEL HARRELL.
Illustrations by CAROLINE CHOE.
Typesetting by WYNNE AU-YEUNG.
Typeset in Helvetica Neue LT Pro.

Consuming raw meats, seafood, poultry, or eggs might increase
your risk of foodborne illness. Please take care when handling and
consuming these ingredients.

10 9 8 7 6 5 4 3 2

Chronicle books and gifts are available at special quantity discounts to
corporations, professional associations, literacy programs, and other
organizations. For details and discount information, please contact our
premiums department at corporatesales@chroniclebooks.com or at
1-800-759-0190.

CHRONICLE BOOKS LLC
680 Second Street
San Francisco, California 94107
www.chroniclebooks.com

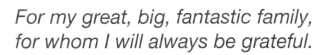

For my great, big, fantastic family,
for whom I will always be grateful.

For my dear students,
follow your hopes and dreams.
This one is for you!

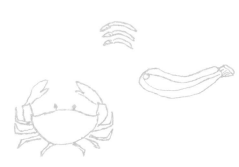

Contents

(part 1) BANCHAN CLASSICS

(part 2) BANCHAN FROM MY KITCHEN

Foreword

Over the last fifteen years, I've navigated the roles of television showrunner, director, and producer, shaping the narratives of travel documentary series, including *Take Out with Lisa Ling* and *Anthony Bourdain: Parts Unknown*. And if there's one thing I've learned in my travels in search of lesser-told stories, it's that the real magic often happens away from the spotlight. It's found in the side streets, in the basements of unmarked buildings, and in the hidden alleys of culture and cuisines. It materializes often, every day, and in plain sight, but usually, it's ignored. Through these pursuits, I've come across remarkable individuals who might initially appear as sidekicks or supporting characters but whose resonance extends far beyond that first encounter.

Enter Caroline Choe, a relentless devotee to this shared passion of uplifting the overlooked, a fervent champion for the unsung, the underestimated, and the seemingly ordinary. My introduction to the force that is Caroline was through Instagram. To be honest, I can't pinpoint the exact moment I met her through her account because, before I had a chance to process, she struck me like a dizzying whirlwind. Her presence was seemingly everywhere. If not there in person, she was online in the comments, uplifting filmmakers, musicians, bakers, writers, painters, chefs, family-owned businesses, and her own kin—an ensemble of everyday heroes, with every cause or instance of good taste deserving her recognition and support.

One look at her stories on social media and you'll see what I mean: snapshots from a bake sale to help reopen the first Asian American bookstore in New York's Chinatown; a video of her congratulating her friend Peter Sohn on the premiere of his new film; a video of a kids' baking class she's overseeing. Dinner with Korean American comedian and podcaster Youngmi Mayer and her son; dinner with her parents; her toasting milestones with her friends. A photo from a sunset celebration for AAPI month; another smiling photo at a performance with musical theater composer Julia Riew; yet another smiling photo but now at a different gala to support Asian American women–led arts and culture projects. A carousel of photos with OG Korean YouTuber Maangchi and the *New York Times*'s Eric Kim. And oh, Latinx and Asian American all-girl punk band The Linda Lindas are in town? You better believe Caroline's already shared a video with them wishing them a warm NYC welcome. The list goes on and on and on. I even recently went to the Bronx to direct a short film on Lloyd's Carrot Cake, an understated NYC gem. I walked into the store, only to find a photo of Caroline and the owner alongside an article she had written highlighting them.

Of course, Caroline has been here.

The woman *shows up*. For everyone.

It's kind of maddening, really. How many places can one person be? How many things can one person do? How many people can one person thoughtfully uplift? Hers is a tireless enthusiasm I could only aspire to. But that is Caroline, supporting and cheering us all on.

It's fitting, then, that Caroline, unwavering in her desire to bring others center stage, decided to make her debut cookbook about banchan, an array of side dishes with a constant, supportive, but often overlooked presence at any Korean dining table.

This book you are holding in your hands is more than just a collection of banchan recipes; it's evidence of Caroline's essence, her very being and capacity to bring the overlooked to the forefront. In these pages, at last, Caroline steps into the spotlight, radiating passion for each and every banchan she's co-signed—these underappreciated dishes that are essential in elevating every meal. Here, she invites us into her personal gallery of flavors, putting her culinary heart on display by sharing closely guarded recipes from her parents as well as recipes from her own kitchen—distinctively Caroline takes on Korean classics.

So take a seat at Caroline's table, where banchan reigns supreme. And let it be a reminder that, sometimes, it is these unsung heroes that steal the show and damn well deserve more celebration and attention than the centerpieces/biggest dishes on the table.

Helen Cho
@helencho
Showrunner/filmmaker
New York City

Introduction

About Banchan

Though banchan—the plethora of small shared sides served with a Korean meal—have often been seen as the supporting cast to the main dish, the colorful extra touches to a big Korean BBQ meal, these dishes are really the ones to remember. The use of banchan dates back to the mid–Three Kingdoms period in Korean history (AD 57 to AD 668). This period was heavily influenced by Buddhism, which meant that eating less meat was the name of the game. Meat was also scarce, and the push for less meat consumption lasted until the Mongol invasions of the thirteenth century. Agriculture became the foundation of eating, as well as dishes that supplemented a bowl of rice—enter banchan. Though banchan came out of a need for survival and preservation, these dishes are now a defining part to a full Korean meal.

Today, the realm of varieties and ingredients within banchan have expanded, with whole shops now devoted to selling exclusively banchan items. The complementary collective of side dishes is now taking center stage, and it's time to celebrate them and their longstanding integral role in Korean cuisine.

Everyone has a personal story behind their go-to banchan selections. Some prefer the classic dishes, while others are embracing modern renditions. Whether made by your own hands, enjoyed in a restaurant, or bought in a store, banchan enhances family-style eating and has become a foundation of its own.

There are technically three main types of banchan to consider: preserved/fermented; muchim (with fresh vegetables); and jorim (soy sauce–braised) and soy sauce–marinated. But there are many other types of preparation: stir-fries, soups, wraps, pancakes, and more, all of which help balance a meal.

Banchan also finds much of its variation through seasonal agriculture and time of year. Growing up Korean American, my family learned to make do with whatever ingredients were in season and available in the outskirts of New York City. I know my parents and older relatives share a chuckle about how, these days, banchan sometimes takes on a new face with popular vegetables in the United States, such as cauliflower and kale. Banchan will look different coming out of my kitchen versus my mom's versus yours, and that's part of its value: all the possibilities that it brings to the table.

One thing I know to be true is that there is much love to be had surrounding banchan, both in terms of making and eating it. Its very nature invites sharing, community, and conversation. While the recipes in this book reflect many of my family's favorites and the dishes I now make in my own kitchen, there is so much more banchan to go around, and I encourage you to explore further. May this book contribute to great times ahead, and most of all, more joyful meals together!

Welcome to My Kitchen

Well, hello there!

My name is Caroline. I'm a Korean American woman, chef, artist, teacher, and writer. I'm a lifelong New Yorker with an awesome Jersey-boy husband; I'm a child of the suburbs and adult of the city; and I have had a life in food that has led me to countless delicious moments, both literally and figuratively!

Though my professional beginnings were in art and education, cooking and food were always in the background. It took a long time for me to finally arrive at the idea that food, cooking, the arts, and teaching about all of them was where I was going to find my life's most fulfilling work. However, I always saw similarities in my approaches to food and art. Just as a studio is a space an artist creates in, a kitchen is where a cook's drive finds action.

In any apartment I have moved into, I have considered the kitchen another room of my own (and my husband can attest to this). It's the room I've taken the most care of, cleaned the most, and probably looked after more closely and intently than my own bedroom. Though many of my New York City apartment kitchens have been small, I made the most of them and made sure they were somewhere I wanted to spend time. They say sometimes the best things come in small packages, and in this

case, it was true! I always try to emphasize to my cooking students that you don't need a big fancy kitchen to make great food. Somehow, the tiniest kitchen I ever had is ultimately where I became a chef, launched a culinary career, and learned that a small space can still feed many.

It helps that, growing up, my family kitchen was not what megawatt kitchens look like today, but it had everything we ever needed. More importantly, it helped lay the first bricks of my culinary groundwork.

My relationship with Korean food has evolved throughout my adult life. In my younger years, I definitely had a preference for "American" food, but just as that term itself is being redefined, so is my relationship to and appreciation for both Korean and Korean American food. (We don't use that dreaded F-word in my kitchen: *fusion*. All food is authentically its own entity.)

Beginning a career in culinary education in 2011 became the gateway to creating more food with the flavors and familiar comfort that I'd known my whole life. This is also when I began making banchan dishes at home, serving them at events and teaching my students how to make them. I experimented with everything from the simple and classic banchan recipes to modern and inventive takes based on how I liked them. Still, all of my cooking had a throughline: Whether it was fresh and quickly made or a dish that took more time and care, all of my recipes created balanced meals and carried on traditions both old and new.

At the same time, the world's approach to Korean food was also evolving—a result, perhaps, of the Korean government making a very large investment in popularizing its exports and culture to the United States.

The population of Koreans and Korean descendants living in the United States grew substantially and continues to grow. As Americans increasingly placed more attention on food and wellness, probiotics, fermentation, and good gut bacteria, they began turning to Korean food and other cuisines that have promoted these foods and values for the ages. The face of the American table was changing, and the conversation about what food was represented on it was finally opening up.

The treatment of kimchi alone can attest to this! America has seemingly fallen more in love with kimchi in recent years, with its avid presence in American supermarkets (much to the amusement of many Koreans). It has become the most popular and defining banchan item, and rather than being treated like typical pickled vegetables, has gained a reputation akin to those of fine wines and cheeses! It has definitely reached new heights since my parents' early days in America, starting in 1973, when kimchi was a rare and expensive thing to find around New York City, and sauerkraut with hot sauce was the only close alternative.

In fact, the folks I've seen who are most in awe of how far the banchan journey has come in their Korean American lives are definitely my mom and dad. Growing up, my siblings and I would accompany them (begrudgingly, heh) on long drives from our home in Westchester, New York, over to the H Marts in Queens and New Jersey, where they would stock up on tons of different ingredients needed to make banchan and other Korean dishes (and if there was a sale on any items, we'd be set for months!). They now marvel at the wide availability of Korean ingredients, the ubiquity of banchan, and the different interpretations of dishes made by younger generations. Most of all, they're amazed at how banchan has been embraced by a much wider audience.

So when I told them that I would be writing a cookbook about Korean American banchan, it began a *whole* conversation—with them and many others. There is so much more to banchan than just kimchi alone, and this book is another way to show that to people everywhere.

When I started brainstorming for this book, I quickly realized it would have to focus on Korean *American* banchan, rather than traditional Korean recipes. Why? Because that's who I am, and that's the kind of food I make in my kitchen. Traditional Korean banchan is part of my life, but I also wanted to contribute something else. As with all American immigrant populations, the Korean American community adds important perspective and diversity to the ongoing conversation about what the American table looks like, and elevates flavors and dishes that are helping change the definition of American food. Food may build a bridge between all of us, but communication and understanding are the bolts that will hold it all together. The expansion of banchan is only helping add our own mark, and sharing my recipes is just one of the things I hope to do to support the cause!

In this book I share stories about growing up Korean American, which I'll bet many readers from other American immigrant families can relate to. I think it's important to share not only the heritage of my family's food, but also all the new and exciting ways it's evolving, as well as the stories behind the people who are helping make that evolution happen.

As for the recipes, picking what to include was just a tad overwhelming! There are so many options in the realms of just jorim, muchim, and fermented vegetables, let alone others like buchimgae (pancakes) and other small dishes. Banchan has a lot to offer! I can only describe it by making an analogy: I was like an artist looking at a very large blank canvas. There was so much to consider and be excited about, but where to start?

Though cheesy (and I can hear some of you groaning already), it really came down to asking these questions: What do I love? What does everyone else around me love? Love really was going to be the answer here.

I started asking many friends and folks around me what their favorite banchan was, and the responses frequently included some of the most classic and simple dishes. My sister Kathy's was gosari namul (fiddlehead fernbrakes); my father's was doenjang guk (fermented soybean paste stew); a few friends named theirs—kkakdugi (cubed radish kimchi), gyeran jiim (steamed eggs), geotjeori (fresh kimchi), and something as simple as gim (dried seaweed sheets). Truly, no one took this question as seriously as my own family members, and they had a hard time choosing a favorite!

The responses I got became my jumping-off point and helped me decide what I would ultimately put in this book. In the end, in addition to recipes for the classic banchan I grew up eating, I also included my own Korean American banchan recipes, as well as other shared dishes and delightful additions to a bapsang (table setup), such as soups and stews.

I know there are probably a few Korean folks out there who might want to come at me to exclaim, "Soups and stews aren't banchan!" While I understand this protective response, which I'll admit is somewhat warranted, I ask them to hear me out as to why I chose to include a handful of soup and stew recipes in this book.

I believe a good soup or stew has a dual identity as both a main and a side dish. Though many Korean soups can stand on their own, I selected a few simple, classic recipes for soups that are frequently featured as shareable dishes or side dishes in Korean restaurants. You'll see them served bubbling hot out of a small earthenware pot, everyone digging in with their spoons. Other times, the shared soup will be ladled into smaller bowls for everyone to enjoy alongside a main. You might also see soups sipped out of a small container or cup with a carryout lunch of different banchan and rice. So, though not a traditional banchan per se, soups and stews can certainly be treated as a side, and that's how I've thought of them for the purposes of this book. And hey, if Maangchi suggests serving some soups and stews as side dishes, who can argue with that? The queen has spoken!

Ultimately, every recipe here came out of love. They're ones I love sharing with my family and friends, teaching my students to make, and the ones everyone has told me (and shown me!) that they have enjoyed eating time and time again. I hope you love them and love sharing them too!

Most of all, my hope is that ultimately this book gets you into the kitchen to have fun creating food, because with banchan, the choices are endless.

Always (or as Much as Possible!) in My Pantry and Fridge

Due to my chef work and home cooking, my pantry is ever evolving as I constantly test out new food items. I have learned a lot over the years, and in writing this list, was honest with myself about what items I consistently use versus those that are just fun to have around. Here are the pantry items I recommend having on hand for all your Korean American banchan-making needs.

BROTH & STOCK

Nothing beats homemade broth and stock, which are rich, fresh, and essential for deepening flavors and providing a foundation for dishes. However, a good boxed version will do in a pinch. I rely on **chicken, vegetable, and a good Korean beef bone broth** (Bibigo is our favorite brand and tastes just like my parents' home-made beef bone broth!).

CANNED & DRIED BEANS, LEGUMES & GRAINS

All of these items go a long way. I try to stock at least one of each of the following at all times: **a bag of rolled oats; a can each of black beans, dark red kidney beans, navy beans, and chick-peas; a bag of lentils; and a bag of quinoa**. All of them provide a good amount of protein and fiber, and the possibilities for reinvention are endless!

CANNED & DRIED FISH

Fresh fish is wonderful, but canned and dried fish are essential for Korean cooking. You can make small, delicious banchan dishes from just the brininess and meaty offerings of each. **Tuna** is always a simple pry-open-and-go meal option, and you can easily create a great small dish with tuna—**tinned smoked oysters** work, as well. **Oil-packed anchovies** offer saltiness and flavor when cooked with garlic, while **dried anchovies** can be used to flavor broth, enjoyed as a crunchy snack, or even blitzed into anchovy powder. One last staple is a bottle of **Korean anchovy sauce**, a fermented sauce made from anchovies and salt, essential for making homemade kimchi. I like the CJ Foods brand. Substitute fish sauce for a similar flavor.

CHEESES

Cheese is a fantastic complement to Korean American cuisine. Funky cheese and funky kimchi are basically cousins, and together they make tasty magic. Among my favorites are a good block of **aged Cabot Cheddar** and a log of **goat cheese** from Vermont Creamery. Some good grated **pecorino** and **fresh mozzarella** work well with fermented flavors. And don't forget about **Kraft American cheese singles**, because sometimes you need them melted over kimchi, or between bread with kimchi for the perfect grilled cheese!

DISPOSABLE FOOD PREP GLOVES

A box of **plastic gloves** is essential for prep and cooking in my kitchen. Though a lot of chefs prefer to wear nitrile or vinyl gloves in the kitchen when preparing food, the gloves I usually choose for my kitchen are polyethylene, which are loose, good for light-duty cooking prep, and latex- and powder-free. These will be instrumental in helping you mix banchan (especially kimchi) more thoroughly than you ever could with a fork or spoon. Gloves will protect your food from any contamination and your skin from any oils and acids.

DRIED SEAWEED, KELP, MUSHROOMS & HONDASHI

There will always be gim (seaweed) in my life (my beloved!). For **seaweed sheets**, I keep a thick and durable option to use for rolls, usually Sushihane or Kwangcheonkim (a.k.a. KIMNORI), both of which are available in many grocery stores and easily found online. I also keep roasted sheets on hand for both snacking and eating with rice. My favorite brand for nibbling is HAIO's premium green laver roasted seaweed. Finally, **dried miyeok strands**, chock-full of nutrients and ready for rehydration at any point for soup or salad, are good to stock.

Dried kelp is useful for building a good, briny broth. Dried mushrooms also offer up plenty of earthiness and concentrated flavor, especially **dried shiitakes, creminis, or porcinis**.

My parents' pantry always had **Ajinomoto's hondashi** in it when I was growing up, and now so does mine. A Japanese seasoning that provides a shortcut to making delicious stock, **hondashi** elevates the umami factor of any broth or liquid it is added to, as it contains dried bonito flakes and, yes, monosodium glutamate, a.k.a. MSG!

FLOURS

The types of flour in my household have increased in recent years, but every single one gets used. Consider which you'll use frequently, and adjust accordingly! For making banchan, I suggest three types: **all-purpose flour, sweet rice flour, and potato flour**. The density of all-purpose flour means it's good for making jeon (pancake), while rice and potato flours are ideal for breading before frying, as they create a light, crispy texture.

FRUIT

When it comes to fruit, I will always raid the supermarket or local farmers' market for **seasonal produce**. Fruit tastes *so* much better when it's in season, so it's best to see what's popping off at the market. That said, it's helpful to stock **lemons, oranges, limes, and other citrus fruit** year-round for cooking and food prep, or to eat on their own, and the scent is absolutely heavenly. Oh yes, and for cocktails!

GREEN TEAS & BORICHA

We always have plenty of tea in stock in my home, including **Korean and Japanese green teas and boricha** (Korean barley tea, my favorite). I keep tea in many forms: loose tea leaves, tea bags, culinary powder, and bottled tea for when we're on the go or, for the best reason, picnicking!

GREEN VEGGIES

In terms of green veggies, **broccoli** is always good to have on hand, since it pairs well with most dishes and is easy to prepare. Also, I always keep two leafy greens in my fridge: **spinach and romaine lettuce**. You can easily make spinach into Shigeumchi Namul (page 48), or use it raw in a green smoothie. Romaine lettuce is hearty and can be easily made not only into salad but also into a quick Geotjeori (Fresh Kimchi, page 54) as well. My husband and I will eat the greens throughout the week, and it makes us feel like responsible, healthy adults!

NOODLES

Dried pasta (ridged penne, cavatappi, or long noodles) and a stash of **ramen noodle packs** are some of the best items to have on standby, as you can make a lot out of a little.

OILS & FATS

Most recipes in this book call for "cooking oil," by which I typically mean vegetable and grapeseed oil, both flavorless with a high smoke point. Here are the fats I keep on hand:

- **Vegetable oil:** Great for frying because of its high smoke point, and pretty common in Korean cooking

- **Grapeseed oil:** A flavorless cooking oil option for frying, with a high smoke point, if you don't have vegetable oil

- **Extra-virgin olive oil:** I recommend having a good-quality EVOO for salad dressings, and another one specifically for pan-frying or other heated cooking

- **Toasted sesame oil:** For flavor, even for frying an egg (the aroma is amazing, and the short cooking time means that the oil won't burn)

- **Bacon or pork fat:** Keep strained drippings in an airtight jar in your fridge or freezer. It's great to have for deepening flavor for any rice dishes and searing of meat before braises. However, pork fat does have a low smoke point, so be aware and maybe remember to turn on your kitchen fan!

RICE

I grew up with **white, sticky short-grain rice** as my household and community staple, though these days I only have it once in a while, usually choosing **short-grain brown rice** as my go-to for more nutrients. I'll use **jasmine rice** for bigger rice-centric dishes.

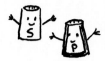

SALT & PEPPER

Salt and pepper are the backbone of most dishes, and are a must for every household pantry. Even when you're working with other bold, strong flavors, you still need salt and pepper. I usually go with a big box of **Diamond Crystal kosher salt**, and I refill my salt jar as needed. I keep plenty of **ground black pepper** on hand for quick seasoning use, as well as **whole black peppercorns**, which I use in broths and brines, or toast then freshly grind to use in a spice blend or finish a dish.

SOY SAUCE (GANJANG)

I didn't grow up with those small bottles of soy sauce—we kept a very large tin in a cabinet. Later in life, I realized how useful this is when you use a lot of soy sauce! Different East Asian cultures use different brewing methods for soy sauce, and I encourage you to find a Korean brand. There are lots to choose from; Haioreum (a.k.a. HAIO) and Sempio are very popular ones. In general, I prefer a traditional **fermented soy sauce** that doesn't have a lot of additives.

SPICES, PASTES & CONDIMENTS

A good collection of spices, pastes, and condiments holds a lot of power, as each one can transform and elevate dishes big or small.

For delicious and spicy heat, you'll need **gochugaru** (Korean dried chili flakes) and **gochujang** (fermented chili paste). For an added depth of bold flavor, I stock **doenjang** (Korean fermented soybean paste) and **shiro** (Japanese white miso paste).

Toasted sesame seeds garnish many dishes with a slight nuttiness. **Dijon mustard** creates tangy marinades and works as a good emulsifying base for sauces and dressings.

Last, my favorite quartet of spices, which adds warmth to many dishes in my house: **onion powder, garlic powder, smoked paprika, and mustard powder**.

SUGARS & SWEETENERS

Sweeteners actually serve more purposes than just to sweeten a dish or add flavor. Properties in sugars act as natural tenderizers to meat and work as browning agents. **White granulated or raw sugar** aids marination and flavor, and **dark brown sugar** provides a molasses flavor in marinades and sauces. Korean recipes sometimes call for honey powder, but I usually just use some **runny honey** or a spoonful of good-quality raw honey. A **light agave nectar syrup** and a good quality **maple syrup** are also great to have and can help make some fantastic sauces!

VEGETABLE AROMATICS

Kimchi by itself is a staple (of course!). Also **yellow onions, fresh garlic, green onions**, and any **in-season alliums** make great aromatics and add tastiness to your dishes, whether served raw, cooked, or yes, fermented!

VINEGARS

Though there are many vinegars used in Asian cooking, I only keep three around at all times. **Distilled white vinegar** is great for marinating and pickling vegetables (and cleaning too!). **Japanese rice wine vinegar** (mirin) is a staple in my house for salad dressings and because it has a sweet, clean taste. I also keep **apple cider vinegar** around for its own sweet, acidic flavor and sometimes home remedy purposes (ACV is good for digestion, wellness, and yes, even home cleaning!).

(part 1) Banchan (

assics

FERMENT

PRESERV

ED &

ED

MOM & DAD'S KIMCHI SERVES 6 TO 8

½ cup [120 ml] cold water

½ Tbsp kosher salt

3 lb [1.4 kg] napa cabbage, rinsed and sliced into 1½ in [4 cm] strips

8 oz [230 g] Chinese daikon radish, peeled and thinly sliced on a mandoline

1 large yellow onion, chopped

1 cup [130 g] chopped green onions, greens and whites

2 Tbsp gochugaru

2 Tbsp anchovy sauce

2 Tbsp minced peeled fresh ginger

1 Tbsp minced garlic

This is the very first recipe my parents ever wrote down for me! If you know, you know: That is a very big deal. My parents never recorded any of their recipes, so this is like pure gold to me. They never measured ingredients; everything was made by taste and from memory—my dad actually once told me, "I am the best cook in this family, and I know what tastes good." (You heard it here first, folks!) They finally sat down to write it out, listing exact measurements based on their preferred flavor and saltiness, and they have stuck to this one recipe for everyday eating and storing in the fridge ever since. When they emailed it to me, I swear I could hear their voices (and yes, they were bickering).

Kimchi is one of those great foods that continues to get funkier with age, so keep this in your refrigerator for several weeks until it's sour and funky, or until it's all gone!

(cont.)

1. In a medium bowl, combine the water and salt, stirring until the salt is mostly dissolved.

2. Combine the cabbage with the salt water, mixing thoroughly so that all the pieces are coated, then let the mixture sit for 3 hours. Give the cabbage a mix once every hour to redistribute the salt water.

3. Drain the cabbage, discarding the salt water, then rinse the cabbage. Taste a piece; if it's very salty, keep rinsing until the saltiness is diluted. Return the rinsed cabbage to the bowl.

4. With gloved hands, add to the bowl the daikon, yellow onion, green onions, gochugaru, anchovy sauce, ginger, and garlic. Use your hands to mix until well combined.

5. Pack the cabbage mixture into a glass storage jar with an airtight lid, leaving 1 in [2.5 cm] of space at the top of the jar.

6. The kimchi can be eaten right away, and while it tastes good fresh, it takes time to become truly delicious. For the best taste, let it ferment in the refrigerator, with the lid on, for 2 weeks, "burping" it every 2 to 3 days (see Notes). Store in your fridge for up to 6 months in an airtight jar. The longer you leave it, the bolder and more sour the flavor will be!

notes: For kimchi storage, look for jars with vents that allow gas to escape during the fermentation process. If you can't find this type of jar, open the jar briefly every 2 or 3 days to allow the kimchi to "burp." If at any point your kimchi comes to room temperature, open your jar carefully over the sink to prevent spillage from a possible eruption from all the fermentation gas!

MOM & DAD'S BAEK KIMCHI
(WHITE KIMCHI) SERVES 6 TO 8

½ cup [120 ml] cold water

½ Tbsp kosher salt

3 lb [1.4 kg] napa cabbage, rinsed and cut into 1½ in [4 cm] square pieces

8 oz [230 g] Chinese daikon radish, peeled and thinly sliced on a mandoline

1 large Asian pear, peeled, seeded, and finely chopped

1 Tbsp chopped green onion, greens and whites

1 Tbsp minced garlic

1 tsp minced peeled fresh ginger

Pine nuts, for garnish

This is the non-spicy version of kimchi. The way my parents make it is not really a "traditional" recipe, but because it's theirs, it's the one I will always like the most!

There are many ways to prepare baek kimchi, but my parents have reasons for using this method. My father told me he doesn't put in any anchovy sauce because the texture "gets too thick," and he prefers not to put in any carrots or too many additional items because they "change the color and flavor." My mother likes to garnish it with the pine nuts rather than age them with the kimchi. In fact, there was a great, loud debate between them about how each prefers their baek kimchi recipe over the other's. If you want to know how adamantly each fought for their opinion on the matter: One parent decided to call me on the landline to convince me as the other *texted* me their opinion!

This is the recipe the two of them landed on in diplomatic agreement.

(cont.)

1. In a medium bowl, combine the water and salt, stirring until the salt is mostly dissolved.

2. Combine the cabbage with the salt water, mixing thoroughly so that all the pieces are coated, then let the mixture sit for 3 hours. Give the cabbage a mix once every hour to redistribute the salt water.

3. Drain the cabbage, discarding the salt water, then rinse the cabbage well. Return the rinsed cabbage to the bowl.

4. With gloved hands, add to the bowl the daikon, Asian pear, green onion, garlic, and ginger. Use your hands to mix until well combined.

5. Pack the cabbage mixture into a glass storage jar with an airtight lid.

6. The kimchi can be eaten right away: Garnish it with the pine nuts and serve. However, it takes time to become truly delicious. For the best taste, let it ferment in the refrigerator, with the lid on, for 2 weeks, "burping" it every 2 to 3 days (see Notes). It will not taste good during the fermentation process, so either eat it fresh, or, for best results, be patient and wait the full 2 weeks! Store the fermented baek in an airtight container in the refrigerator for up to 1 month.

notes: For kimchi storage, look for jars with vents that allow gas to escape during the fermentation process. If you can't find this type of jar, open the jar briefly every 2 or 3 days to allow the kimchi to "burp." If at any point your kimchi comes to room temperature, open your jar carefully over the sink to prevent spillage from a possible eruption from all the fermentation gas!

KKAENIP JANGAJJI (SPICY PICKLED PERILLA LEAVES) SERVES 6 TO 8

32 perilla leaves

Kosher salt

½ cup [120 ml] soy sauce

5 garlic cloves, minced

1 Tbsp sugar or honey

1 Tbsp gochugaru

2 green onions, green and white parts finely chopped

1 chile (green or red), thinly sliced

Kkaenip, or perilla leaves, are tender and have an almost minty taste, and you'll often find them featured in Korean cooking. Though they usually have green leaves, the best kkaenip I ever tried was dark purple and harvested straight from my friend's father's garden!

This versatile leaf can be steamed, fried in oil, or even cooked in jeon (pancake). My family often ate it at dinner with different banchan, rice, and some delicious grilled meat.

Many folks, including my brother, Patrick, prepare their own kkaenip jangajji with homegrown kkaenip, since it can grow very avidly in one's yard. However, if you're without a yard, you can find kkaenip at your local Asian grocery store. Make sure to look for fresh leaves that aren't yet wilted or brown.

1   Rinse the perilla leaves carefully in a colander under cold water. Shake off any excess water, then pat the perilla leaves dry with paper towels. Toss the leaves with a light seasoning of salt, and set aside.

2   In a small bowl, combine the soy sauce, garlic, sugar, gochugaru, green onions, and sliced chile. Mix well until the sugar dissolves.

3   Lay one perilla leaf in a glass storage container with a tight-fitting lid. Spread the top of the leaf evenly with about 1 Tbsp of the soy sauce mixture, and stack another leaf on top. Repeat until all the leaves are stacked and covered.

4   Secure the lid on the container and store it in the fridge for 24 hours. The kkaenip jangajji can be eaten after that 24 hours, but for a more pickled flavor, store for 3 days before serving. Kkaenip can be stored in an airtight container in the refrigerator for up to 1 week.

OI MUCHIM (SPICY CUCUMBER SALAD) SERVES 2 TO 4

3 Persian or Kirby cucumbers, thinly sliced

Kosher salt

1 Tbsp white vinegar

1 Tbsp soy sauce

1 Tbsp sugar

2 tsp gochugaru

2 tsp toasted sesame oil

½ tsp hondashi

1 garlic clove, minced

1 green onion, green and white parts chopped

Toasted sesame seeds, crushed or whole, for garnish

Over the years, I've noticed that many Americans have become fans of oi muchim. I suppose the popularity goes hand in hand with the widespread and growing appreciation for kimchi. Their spiciness is similar, but oi muchim has the added refreshing coolness of cucumber. There is nothing like homemade oi muchim, and I encourage everyone to give it a try! My parents have their version, but this is mine, with a touch of their personal preference: using hondashi instead of fish sauce.

1 In a small bowl, add the cucumbers and give the slices a light seasoning of salt all over. Let sit for about 10 minutes to draw out excess moisture. Drain and discard any liquid.

2 In a separate small bowl, combine the vinegar, soy sauce, sugar, 2 tsp of salt, gochugaru, sesame oil, hondashi, garlic, and green onion. Stir well until the sugar is dissolved.

3 Pour the sauce over the cucumbers in the bowl and mix until everything is coated.

4 Garnish with sesame seeds and serve immediately, or store in the refrigerator (without sesame seeds) for up to 1 week.

KKAKDUGI
(CUBED RADISH KIMCHI) ^{SERVES 4 TO 6}

2 lb [910 g] Chinese daikon radish, peeled and cut into 1 to 2 in [2.5 to 5 cm] cubes

Kosher salt

5 garlic cloves, minced

3 green onions, green and white parts finely chopped

½ cup [65 g] gochugaru

3 Tbsp anchovy sauce

1½ Tbsp sugar

1 tsp grated peeled fresh ginger

I can call to mind the distinct crunching of someone enjoying kkakdugi with a meal. Bright and crisp, this pickled daikon radish kimchi goes so well with a bowl of gomtang (beef bone soup) and rice, a comfort meal for many.

There are a few family touches to this recipe. Because Korean mu (daikon radish) is a big vegetable, I prefer using Chinese mu, which is longer and more slender. Its smaller size is perfect when cooking for just my two-person household.

Though usually folks will add rice flour to their recipes to aid fermentation, my parents don't love the texture it gives. The natural fermentation that sugar offers has always been good enough for them, and in fact, they advise everyone to rely on the trusty yangnyeom seasoning combination to make it taste good: gochugaru, garlic, ginger, and sugar.

1   In a medium bowl, add the daikon and season the cubes with salt, tossing to combine. Let sit overnight or for 24 hours.

2   Strain the daikon, reserving the excess liquid in a small bowl. Set aside.

3   Rinse the cubes of excess salt, and return the cubes to the bowl.

4   With gloved hands, add to the bowl the garlic, green onions, gochugaru, anchovy sauce, sugar, ginger, and 1 Tbsp of the reserved daikon liquid. Mix until all the cubes are coated.

5   Transfer the daikon to a glass storage container and secure with an airtight lid. Leave out at room temperature for about 24 hours before serving. Or store in the refrigerator for 3 to 4 days before serving. Kkakdugi can be stored in an airtight container in the fridge for up to 3 months.

DAD'S SOY SAUCE PICKLES

½ cup [120 ml] soy sauce

¼ cup [60 ml] apple cider vinegar

2 Tbsp sugar

1 tsp hondashi

3 Persian or Kirby cucumbers

As a New Yorker, I have had the pleasure of indulging in every kind of deli pickle imaginable. You've got your sours, half sours, gherkins, bread and butter—we're a tad spoiled in that regard!

My dad has a few pickle recipes of his own, but this is the one that seems to complement every meal he prepares. When I learned how to make them for myself, I approached them a little differently, but I still remember his whimsical tips and instructions. For instance, he's a fan of shaking your pickle jar right away to let the flavors get acquainted, and then shaking it again after twenty-four hours. However, I'm a fan of letting the cucumbers sit and do their pickling thing. I will choose to be diplomatic and say you can do it either way, because they will still be great soy sauce pickles in the end!

1   In a small pot over medium heat, combine the soy sauce, vinegar, sugar, and hondashi with 1 cup [240 ml] of water, whisking until the sugar and hondashi dissolve. Remove the pickling liquid from the heat and pour it into a heatproof measuring cup or small bowl. Set aside to cool.

2   Cut each cucumber lengthwise into quarters, then cut each quarter lengthwise in half. (You will have eight spears from each cucumber.)

3   Put all the small cucumber spears into a glass jar. Pour the pickling liquid over the cucumbers, then secure the lid. Once the jar has cooled completely, transfer the jar to the refrigerator. My dad says the pickles can be eaten as early as 24 hours later. However, a more concentrated taste will develop after 3 to 4 days. Try them at both stages to determine which you like! Pickles can be refrigerated in an airtight jar for up to 2 weeks.

GOCHU JANGAJJI (SPICY PICKLED CHILES) SERVES 4 TO 6

½ cup [120 ml] soy sauce

¼ cup [60 ml] white vinegar

2 Tbsp kosher salt

1 Tbsp sugar

1 tsp honey

1 lb [455 g] cheong gochu (green chiles)

Korean green chiles were a constant presence in my household fridge growing up. You could smell the spiciness in the air whenever they were being cooked. For those seeking great flavor and a kick to their meal, gochu jangajji checks those boxes.

I had friends in college who absolutely craved these chiles late at night. They pair well with a late-night pizza or a bowl of rice from your dorm room rice cooker (if that's all you can manage to whip up at 2 a.m.).

Some folks will boil the brine again after its initial 24 hours of pickling (removing the chiles before boiling and then resubmerging them in the liquid) to ensure chiles that last for months. However, I leave them to pickle in the fridge after the first standing and they're still delicious. Totally up to you!

1   In a medium pot over medium-low heat, combine the soy sauce, vinegar, salt, sugar, and honey with 2 cups [480 ml] of water, stirring until the sugar dissolves. Allow the liquid to come to a boil, then turn off the heat and set aside to cool down a bit.

2   If you'd like, trim the tops off the chiles. Using a toothpick or fork, poke the chiles all over their surfaces (to allow for the brine to seep in). Place the poked chiles into a glass jar that can hold about 3 cups [720 ml] of liquid.

3   Pour the brining liquid over the chiles in the jar and secure the lid. Let the jar sit at room temperature in your kitchen for about 24 hours.

4   After the initial 24-hour waiting period, store in the refrigerator for 3 to 5 days before serving—3 if you absolutely can't wait, and 5 if you'd like a deeper flavor. Chiles can be stored in an airtight jar in the refrigerator for up to 1 month.

SSAMJANG (SPICY DIPPING SAUCE) _{SERVES 4}

2 Tbsp doenjang

1 Tbsp gochujang

1 Tbsp toasted sesame oil

2 tsp honey

1 tsp toasted sesame seeds

1 garlic clove, minced

1 green onion, green and white parts finely chopped

Ssamjang is one of those reliable sauces that adds the right finishing touch to your lettuce wrap full of rice and barbecued meat. It's spicy and sweet, and takes just a bit of this and that to create. A little goes a long way.

1   In a small bowl, combine the doenjang, gochujang, sesame oil, honey, sesame seeds, garlic, and green onion, stirring well with a fork until fully combined. Serve as a dipping sauce alongside rice, vegetables, and broth, or my personal favorite, KBBQ meat. If storing, cover in plastic wrap or store in an airtight container for up to 3 days.

NAMUL &
(Fresh Veg

MUCHIM
etables)

SHIGEUMCHI NAMUL (SEASONED SPINACH SALAD) SERVES 2 TO 4

1 lb [455 g] fresh spinach, rinsed and blanched

1 garlic clove, minced

2 tsp toasted sesame oil

1 tsp toasted sesame seeds, plus more for garnish

½ tsp kosher salt

¼ tsp ground black pepper

1 green onion, green and white parts finely chopped

Pinch of sugar

I credit shigeumchi namul for my early love of spinach. It's a perfect balance of saltiness, softness, and just a little bite of freshness. Some folks add their own touches—a little doenjang or gochugaru or even a touch of anchovies—but it's also excellent with just a few seasonings.

Make sure that you blanch, and do not boil, your spinach. You still want it to have a little bit of bite and not be too mushy!

1   In a medium bowl, combine the blanched spinach, garlic, sesame oil, sesame seeds, salt, pepper, green onion, and sugar. Mix thoroughly with a fork or a gloved hand.

2   Cover the bowl with plastic wrap and let it chill in the fridge for 20 to 30 minutes before serving. Garnish with sesame seeds. Leftovers can be stored in an airtight container in the refrigerator for up to 3 days.

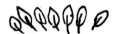

KONGNAMUL MUCHIM (SOYBEAN SPROUT SALAD) SERVES 2 TO 4

1 lb [455 g] soybean sprouts, rinsed and blanched

1 garlic clove, minced

2 tsp toasted sesame oil

1 tsp toasted sesame seeds

½ tsp kosher salt

¼ tsp ground black pepper

1 green onion, green and white parts finely chopped

Pinch of sugar

If Shigeumchi Namul (page 48) was my gateway to loving spinach, kongnamul muchim was my gateway to appreciating bean sprouts. It's a classic, light, and nutritious dish with the right amount of crunch. This can actually be made with many of the same ingredients as shigeumchi namul, so it's almost a two-for-one!

Bold statement, but I will say it loudly and proudly: Both this and shigeumchi namul are my ultimate *favorite* banchan, and I will probably finish both these dishes on any table! Whether enjoyed with KBBQ, added to Bibimbap (page 179), or rolled into Kimbap (page 137), they are undoubtedly my top choices when it comes to banchan.

1   In a medium bowl, combine the soybean sprouts, garlic, sesame oil, sesame seeds, salt, pepper, green onion, and sugar. Mix thoroughly with a fork or a gloved hand.

2   Cover the bowl with plastic wrap and chill for 20 to 30 minutes, or serve immediately. Store in the refrigerator for up to 3 days.

SESAME BROCCOLI SALAD SERVES 4 TO 5

2 broccoli crowns, cut into small florets

2 Tbsp chopped green onion, greens and whites

1 Tbsp toasted sesame oil

1 tsp kosher salt

½ tsp ground black pepper

1 garlic clove, minced

Toasted sesame seeds

Another classic and user-friendly vegetable banchan dish that seems to go with everything! You might ask yourself if my liking broccoli can be credited to it being prepared this way? The answer is a resounding *yes*.

1 To a medium pot or skillet, add just enough water to cover the bottom by about ½ in [13 mm], and bring to a boil over high heat. Lower the heat to medium-high, and add the broccoli florets in an even layer on the bottom. Cover the pot and allow them to steam for 6 minutes, or until tender but still green. Transfer the broccoli to a medium bowl of ice water to shock the florets and stop the cooking. Drain in a colander in the sink. Place the shocked broccoli back in the empty bowl.

2 Add the green onion, sesame oil, salt, pepper, garlic, and a generous sprinkling of sesame seeds. Mix thoroughly with a spoon or a gloved hand.

3 Cover the bowl with plastic wrap and let it chill in the fridge for about 20 minutes before serving. Store leftovers in an airtight container in the refrigerator for up to 3 days.

GEOTJEORI (FRESH KIMCHI) SERVES 4 TO 5

1 small napa cabbage or head of red lettuce, about 1 lb [455 g], rinsed and sliced into pieces 1 or 2 in [2.5 or 5 cm] wide

Kosher salt

2 Tbsp gochugaru

3 garlic cloves, minced

1 tsp grated peeled fresh ginger

2 Tbsp toasted sesame oil

2 green onions, green and white parts chopped

1 Tbsp anchovy sauce

1 tsp white or red wine vinegar

1 tsp sugar

1 tsp ground black pepper

Toasted sesame seeds, for garnish

Geotjeori is a fresh kimchi that can be enjoyed anytime and for any meal. A single-batch recipe with all the elements and flavors of kimchi without the fermentation time, it's the perfect fix for your vegetable needs. This is the recipe my parents passed to me for a classic baechu (napa cabbage) geotjeori.

1 Rinse the cabbage pieces in a colander, shaking off any excess water, and then transfer them to a large bowl. Cover the cabbage with a generous dusting of salt, and let sit for 30 minutes to 1 hour, until the cabbage is beginning to wilt and become liquidy.

2 Drain the cabbage, discarding the excess liquid, and rinse the cabbage in a colander. Squeeze the cabbage to remove as much water as you can, then return it to the bowl. Set aside.

3 In a small bowl, combine the gochugaru, garlic, ginger, sesame oil, green onions, anchovy sauce, vinegar, sugar, and pepper. Stir well until the sugar dissolves.

4 Pour the sauce on top of the cabbage and, with gloved hands, mix until the cabbage pieces are well coated.

5 Garnish with sesame seeds and serve. Store leftovers in an airtight container in the refrigerator for up to 1 week.

PA MUCHIM
(SHAVED GREEN ONION SALAD) SERVES 3 TO 5

5 green onions	2 tsp rice wine vinegar	1 tsp soy sauce
Kosher salt	2 tsp gochugaru	Ground black pepper
1 Tbsp toasted sesame oil	1 tsp sugar	Toasted sesame seeds, for garnish

Best had with a good KBBQ meal, pa muchim is amazing even on a pizza! (See the recipe for Pa Muchim Pizza, page 195.) You could also consider swapping the green onions for ramps during the spring season when ramps are plentifully available.

1   Cut the green onions in half crosswise, then in thin lengthwise strips.

2   Soak the green onions in 2 cups [480 ml] of cold, lightly salted water for about 10 minutes. Drain the green onions, pat them dry with paper towels, and put them in a medium bowl.

3   To the green onions, add the sesame oil, vinegar, gochugaru, sugar, and soy sauce. Toss well with gloved hands until the green onions are thoroughly coated.

4   Season with salt and pepper, garnish with sesame seeds, and serve immediately. Pa muchim can be stored in an airtight container in the refrigerator for up to 3 days; however, keep in mind that it will continue wilting as the days go on and both color and texture will change.

MIYEOK MUCHIM (SEAWEED SALAD) SERVES 4 TO 5

1 oz [30 g] dried miyeok (about 2 cups [200 g] after soaking)

3 Tbsp white or red wine vinegar

2 tsp sugar

2 tsp soy sauce

1 tsp toasted sesame oil

1 tsp toasted sesame seeds, plus more for garnish

1 garlic clove, minced

1 green onion, green and white parts finely chopped

1 Persian or Kirby cucumber, cut into matchsticks

A refreshing salad with plenty of health benefits! As my mother would say, "Miyeok muchim is priceless fiber, and very healthy!"

When soup weather has subsided and you're no longer craving miyeokguk (seaweed soup, such as my Chicken & Oyster Miyeokguk, page 93), this is a terrific dish to feature on the table.

You can find dried miyeok in the dried seaweed section of your local Asian supermarket.

(cont.)

1   In a large bowl, soak the dried miyeok in water according to the package instructions or just until it softens, usually 15 to 20 minutes. Once rehydrated, rinse the miyeok to remove any hidden sand. Drain well in a colander.

2   In a medium pot over high heat, bring about 2 cups [480 ml] of water to a boil. Plunge the miyeok into the water and blanch for 1 minute. Drain and rinse in cold water until the miyeok is cool. Once the miyeok is cool enough to touch, squeeze out the excess water.

3   Chop the miyeok into bite-size pieces.

4   In a medium bowl, combine the vinegar, sugar, soy sauce, sesame oil, sesame seeds, and garlic and mix until the sugar dissolves.

5   Add the miyeok, green onion, and cucumber and toss well. Garnish with more sesame seeds. Serve immediately, or cover with plastic wrap and store for at least 30 minutes in your fridge to serve cold. Some folks even put some ice chips in their miyeok muchim beforehand to serve it extra cold! Refrigerate in a sealed container for up to 5 days.

GOSARI NAMUL (FIDDLEHEAD FERNBRAKE SALAD) SERVES 3 TO 4

1 oz [30 g] dried gosari

1 Tbsp soy sauce

½ Tbsp toasted sesame oil

¼ tsp sugar

1 green onion, green and white parts finely chopped

2 garlic cloves, minced

½ tsp ground black pepper

Cooking oil

1 tsp toasted sesame seeds

When I was asking my family if they could name their favorite banchan, my sister said "gosari namul" without hesitation. Way to go, Kathy!

Gosari namul is made with edible ferns known as fernbrakes or bracken fiddleheads, which traditionally grow in the mountains. They're advertised these days as an earthy superfood. In this recipe, they're seasoned simply with green onions, garlic, and soy sauce. Gosari namul is often served as part of a traditional colorful vegetable plate with Shigeumchi Namul (page 48), Kongnamul Muchim (page 50), and doraji (bellflower root), or along with Bibimbap (page 179) or yukgaejang (spicy beef soup).

It's common to find packaged dried fernbrakes in Asian supermarkets; boil and soak them well beforehand or else the texture might be a little twiggy. In an ever-awesome Korean market that thinks ahead for home cooks, you can now also buy them parboiled. However, I find boiling and soaking fresh fernbrakes at home—still the favored method in my family—result in a less mushy dish.

(cont.)

1   In a large bowl, soak the dried gosari in enough water to completely cover it. Cover the bowl with plastic wrap, and set it aside at room temperature to soak for at least 8 hours or overnight.

2   Drain the gosari, discarding the soaking liquid.

3   In a medium pot over high heat, bring water to a boil. Lower the heat to medium, then add the gosari, cooking them for about 30 minutes. Drain the gosari in a colander and rinse well with cold water. Take this time to comb through them, pulling out any extra-tough excess bits and woody parts off the stems.

4   Chop the gosari into 2 to 3 in [5 to 7.5 cm] pieces and transfer them to a large bowl.

5   In a small bowl, combine the soy sauce, sesame oil, sugar, green onion, garlic, and pepper and mix until the sugar dissolves. Pour this mixture over the gosari and toss well to combine.

6   Set a skillet over medium-high heat and lightly coat the bottom of the pan with cooking oil. Allow the oil to heat for about 1 minute. Add the gosari and cook, stirring, for about 3 minutes. Carefully add ¼ cup [60 ml] of water, turn the heat to low, cover the pan, and cook the gosari for 3 to 5 minutes more or until tender.

7   Transfer the gosari to a serving bowl or plate. Garnish with the sesame seeds and serve right away, or store in an airtight container in the fridge for up to 3 to 4 days.

JORIM & S

SAUCE-M

OY

ARINATED

GAMJA JORIM (SOY-BRAISED POTATOES)

SERVES 4 TO 5

¼ cup [60 ml] soy sauce

1½ Tbsp honey

2 tsp toasted sesame oil

Cooking oil

1 lb [455 g] baby creamer potatoes, rinsed and halved, or 3 large Yukon gold potatoes, chopped into 1 in [2.5 cm] cubes

1 medium yellow onion, diced

3 garlic cloves, minced

Kosher salt

Ground black pepper

1 green Korean chile, sliced (optional)

1 cup [240 ml] low-sodium chicken or mushroom stock

1 green onion, green part only, finely chopped

Toasted sesame seeds, for garnish

Gochugaru (optional), for garnish

Sometimes I can't decide what is more comforting: a soft potato or a bowl of rice. Lucky for me, gamja jorim offers the best of both worlds: These sweet and savory potatoes are wonderful served hot alongside some rice. Or serve them cold in a lunchbox with Mom & Dad's Kimchi (page 28), Shigeumchi Namul (page 48), and Kongnamul Muchim (page 50) for a classic banchan combo! Should you want extra flavor, feel free to add in one chopped green bell pepper or, for a little spiciness, two chopped Korean green chiles.

(cont.)

1   In a small bowl, combine the soy sauce, honey, and sesame oil and stir until the honey dissolves. Set aside.

2   Set a large skillet over medium-high heat and lightly coat the bottom of the pan with cooking oil. Allow the oil to heat for about 2 minutes, or until it shimmers.

3   Carefully add the potatoes to the pan and cook for 4 to 5 minutes, until they start to brown.

4   Add the yellow onion and garlic, and douse them with a generous seasoning of salt and pepper. If using the chile, add it in as well. Stirring with a wooden spatula, cook the vegetables for 2 to 3 minutes, or until the onion is golden brown and translucent.

5   Carefully add the soy sauce mixture, stirring until all the vegetables are well coated with the sauce.

6   Add the chicken stock and bring the liquid to a boil. Cover the pan, turn the heat to medium-low, and simmer the potatoes for about 15 minutes, basting the potatoes halfway through with the braising liquid, until fork-tender. Transfer the potatoes to a serving dish.

7   Garnish with the green onion greens, sesame seeds, and gochugaru (if using), and serve. Store in an airtight container in the refrigerator for up to 5 days.

YUKHOE (SOY-MARINATED RAW BEEF) SERVES 4

½ Tbsp toasted sesame seeds, plus more for garnish

½ Tbsp honey or agave nectar

2 tsp soy sauce

1 tsp toasted sesame oil

1 tsp ground black pepper

1 green onion, green and white parts separated and finely chopped

1 garlic clove, minced

7 oz [200 g] flank steak

¼ Asian pear or ½ Bosc pear, peeled and finely chopped or julienned

1 egg yolk (optional)

As my palate changed as I got older, so did my appreciation for yukhoe. It's beef tartare's Korean sibling, and, when made at its freshest and paired with some hot rice and a raw egg, it can be absolutely delicious. It's a regal dish—apparently yukhoe was mainly served at royal banquets during the Chosun Dynasty. Now you'll often see it served up at some pretty fancy Korean restaurants when made with Hanwoo or Wagyu beef.

When making it in your own home, get a really good-quality, tender cut of beef that's pretty lean; I like flank steak for its texture. For safety precautions, make sure to keep the meat super cold to inhibit any bacteria growth. In fact, to make slicing a bit easier and to aid in keeping your meat cold, stick the meat in the freezer for 20 to 30 minutes before cutting it. Feel free to either chop and mix the pears into the beef mixture, or julienne them and arrange them prettily beneath the beef on a chilled plate. Try it both ways and see which you prefer!

(cont.)

1 In a medium bowl, combine the sesame seeds, honey, soy sauce, sesame oil, pepper, green onion whites, and garlic, mixing well with a fork. Set aside.

2 Using a sharp knife, finely chop the beef, trimming off any excess fat.

3 To the bowl, add the chopped beef, and with a gloved hand or large spoon, carefully mix until the beef is completely coated. Add the chopped pear and mix until just combined, or arrange the julienned pears on a serving plate or bowl, depending on your preference.

4 Transfer the beef mixture to the serving plate or bowl, using your hands to form a round shape. If using the egg yolk, carefully create a small well in the center of the beef with your thumb or the back of a spoon, and place the egg yolk in it.

5 Garnish with more sesame seeds and the green onion greens. Chill the dish in the refrigerator for 30 minutes. Serve cold. This dish should be eaten the day it's made.

DUBU JORIM (SOY-BRAISED TOFU) SERVES 4 TO 5

1½ Tbsp soy sauce

1 Tbsp toasted sesame oil

2 tsp gochugaru

1 tsp toasted sesame seeds

1 tsp sugar or honey

18 oz [510 g] firm tofu, sliced ½ in [13 mm] thick

Cooking oil

2 green onions, green and white parts separated and finely chopped

2 garlic cloves, minced

Whether you're vegetarian, vegan, flexitarian, or anything else besides, dubu jorim is a helpful recipe to have in your back pocket. It's perfect for when you're in the mood for a simple, healthy protein dish, and it's very delicious!

1   In a small bowl, combine the soy sauce, sesame oil, gochugaru, sesame seeds, and sugar with ¼ cup [60 ml] of water, stirring until the sugar dissolves. Set aside.

2   With a paper towel, pat the tofu slices well to remove excess water. Set a nonstick skillet or frying pan over medium-high heat and lightly coat the bottom of the pan with cooking oil. Allow the oil to heat for about 2 minutes. Carefully, with the aid of a spatula to prevent breakage, place the tofu pieces in the pan and cook them on both sides for 3 to 4 minutes each or until golden brown on both sides. Carefully transfer the tofu to a plate and set aside.

3   Add a little more cooking oil to the pan, and let it heat for about 1 minute (it won't take as long because the pan is already hot). Add the green onion whites and garlic, and cook for 4 to 5 minutes, or until just golden brown. Turn the heat down to medium-low and carefully add the sauce to the pan, gently scraping the bottom of the pan with a wooden spatula to lift any delicious brown bits from the onions and garlic.

4   Carefully add the browned tofu slices back to the pan and cover. After about 2 minutes, spoon the pan sauce over the tofu slices a few times. Allow the tofu to simmer for 1 to 3 minutes more, or until the sauce has been mostly absorbed by the tofu.

5   Turn off the heat and transfer the tofu slices to a serving bowl or plate. Garnish with the green onion greens and serve hot right away. Store leftovers in an airtight container in the refrigerator for up to 3 days and have it cold!

DAEGU JORIM (SOY-POACHED COD) SERVES 3 TO 4

2 Tbsp soy sauce

1 Tbsp sugar

1 cup [130 g] Chinese daikon radish cubes, about 1 in [2.5 cm] thick

1 small yellow onion, sliced

2 Korean green chiles, each cut into 3 pieces

2 green onions, green and white parts chopped, plus more for garnish

3 garlic cloves, minced

2 cod fillets, 6 oz [170 g] each, cut into 2 in [5 cm] pieces

There are many jorim (soy sauce–braised) dishes, but this one is my father's favorite. When I asked him how he prepares his daegu jorim, he was adamant about a few preferences he has in preparing it and how he feels it gets the best flavor. I use cod fillets in this recipe, but he prefers to cook with the neck part of the cod for a rich flavor, since cod is a pretty light-tasting fish. He also advises everyone to use the smaller, more slender Chinese mu (daikon radish) instead of Korean daikon radish, for ease of portioning and preparation. He warns, "Just know, a lot of liquid will come out of the mu."

This is a recipe of simple ingredients, but it makes for a classic dish with a balance of both light and bold flavors—and a nice ol' kick!

1   In a small bowl, combine the soy sauce and sugar with 1 cup [240 ml] of water. Stir until all the sugar dissolves.

2   In a shallow pot or Dutch oven, combine the daikon, yellow onion, chiles, green onions, and garlic and spread in an even layer. Place the cod pieces on top of the vegetables, then pour the soy sauce mixture over.

3   Set the pot over medium-high heat, and allow everything to come to a boil (additional liquid will come from the daikon as it cooks).

4   Turn the heat to medium-low and let simmer for 10 to 15 minutes, basting the fish once halfway through, until the daikon is tender and the cod is opaque. Turn off the heat and carefully transfer the fish and vegetables to a serving plate.

5   Coat the fish in spoonfuls of the braising liquid, garnish with green onions, and serve hot. If you have leftovers, store in an airtight container in the refrigerator for up to 2 days.

STIR-FRIE

STEAMED

&

MICROWAVE GYERANJJIM (STEAMED EGGS) SERVES 2 TO 4

3 eggs

½ cup [120 ml] Vegetable Anchovy Broth (page 158) or water

1 tsp toasted sesame oil

½ tsp kosher salt

¼ tsp ground black pepper

½ tsp hondashi (optional)

1 tsp toasted sesame seeds

1 green onion, green part only, finely chopped

Gyeranjjim is the steaming hot fluffy egg custard that you find on the table at Korean barbecue. It can be made at home traditionally, steamed in an earthenware pot, but there's another, easier way to do it, as my family did: in a regular bowl in the microwave!

I'm sure my dad might scoff at how I prepare my gyeranjjim (his classic recipe uses just five ingredients), but hey, he has his way, and I have mine!

1   In a medium microwave-safe serving bowl, combine the eggs, broth, sesame oil, salt, pepper, and hondashi (if using), whisking well with a fork until everything is smooth and fully combined. Sprinkle the sesame seeds and green onion greens on top.

2   Carefully place the bowl in the microwave and cook on high for 3 minutes, uncovered, or until the edges begin to set. (If the egg comes close to the top of the bowl, it can overflow a bit; place a paper towel under the bowl for easier cleanup.)

3   Carefully remove the bowl from the microwave and gently scrape down the sides and bottom with a spoon. Return the bowl to the microwave, and cook for 2 minutes more. Check on the eggs; continue cooking in 45-second intervals until the eggs are set but still soft when poked with a fork.

4   Remove the bowl from the microwave, and allow the eggs to rest for about 5 minutes. Serve hot and right away!

JAPCHAE (STIR-FRIED SWEET POTATO NOODLES) SERVES 4 TO 5

SAUCE

¼ cup [60 ml] soy sauce

2 Tbsp toasted sesame oil

1 Tbsp toasted sesame seeds

½ Tbsp sugar or honey

½ tsp ground black pepper

NOODLES

8 oz [230 g] Korean dangmyeon (sweet potato starch noodles)

1 Tbsp toasted sesame oil

½ Tbsp soy sauce

BEEF

2 Tbsp soy sauce

1 Tbsp toasted sesame oil

½ Tbsp sugar

1 tsp ground black pepper

8 oz [230 g] thinly sliced rib eye

Cooking oil

VEGETABLES

Cooking oil

1 small yellow onion, chopped

2 garlic cloves, minced

1 carrot, cut into matchsticks

½ red bell pepper, sliced

Kosher salt

Ground black pepper

8 oz [230 g] fresh shiitake mushrooms, sliced

2 cups [60 g] fresh spinach

GARNISH

Toasted sesame seeds

So, japchae isn't really considered a banchan dish, but it can work as one when served in small portions at home or divided up at a restaurant. Most often, you see japchae on the table at a special occasion, or these days, even as part of a great meal on the go. I will give my aunts all the props in the world for my appreciation of japchae. I fondly recall the time my eldest aunt took her gloved hand as she was mixing the noodles and veggies with the sauce and fed me a handful straight into my mouth! Now, that is love.

There is an ongoing debate about whether sweetness belongs in japchae; I say it's dealer's choice. If you don't want it sweet, skip the sugar in the sauce and beef. Also, feel free to use another kind of meat, or eliminate the meat and use a sliced egg omelette for a vegetarian version, or more veggies to keep it vegan. No matter how you prepare it, who doesn't love a good stir-fried noodle?

MAKE THE SAUCE:

1   In a small bowl, combine the soy sauce, sesame oil, sesame seeds, sugar, and pepper, stirring until the sugar dissolves. Set aside.

COOK THE NOODLES:

1   Set a large pot with 8 cups [2 L] of water over medium-high heat and bring to a boil. Add the dangmyeon and cook for about 5 minutes, or until the noodles soften and become clear. Drain the noodles in a colander, and transfer to a large bowl. While the noodles are still hot, add the sesame oil and soy sauce and gently toss with tongs to coat the noodles (this adds flavor and also keeps the noodles from sticking together). Set aside.

COOK THE BEEF:

1   In a medium bowl, combine the soy sauce, sesame oil, sugar, and pepper and mix together with the beef.

2   Set a large skillet over medium-high heat and lightly coat the bottom of the pan with cooking oil. Add the beef and cook for 3 to 5 minutes, or until the beef is browned and cooked through.

(cont.)

COOK THE VEGETABLES:

1 Set a large skillet over medium-high heat and lightly coat the bottom of the pan with cooking oil. When the oil is hot, add the onion, garlic, carrot, and bell pepper, and season with salt and pepper. Gently toss with a wooden spatula, and cook until the onion is translucent and golden brown.

2 Add the mushrooms, seasoning with a pinch more of salt, and continue to stir-fry with the other vegetables for about 1 minute— let the mushrooms become tender, but don't overcook them or they'll be slimy.

3 Turn the heat to medium-low, then handful by handful, gradually add the spinach, letting it wilt between handfuls to make space for more spinach. Cook until all of the spinach is wilted.

MAKE THE JAPCHAE:

1 Turn the heat to low, and return the meat and any accumulated juices to the pan, stirring to combine. Add the noodles and stir to fully combine.

2 Pour the sauce over the noodles and gently toss with tongs until everything is coated. Continue cooking the japchae over low heat for 3 minutes, or until the sauce is absorbed into the noodles.

3 Transfer the japchae to a serving dish. Season with more salt and pepper as needed, garnish with sesame seeds, and serve! Store any leftovers in an airtight container in the refrigerator for up to 3 days.

MYEOLCHI BOKKEUM (STIR-FRIED ANCHOVIES) SERVES 2 TO 4

1 Tbsp soy sauce

½ Tbsp toasted sesame oil, plus more for garnish

2 tsp sugar

½ tsp ground black pepper

Cooking oil

2 garlic cloves, minced

4 oz [115 g] small dried anchovies

Toasted sesame seeds, for garnish

There were always dried anchovies in my parents' pantry, and with good reason. They are the backbone of much Korean cooking, adding protein to a meal; they can be whipped up into all kinds of delicious bites when the need strikes, or just snacked on as is. Preparing them this way, with a sweet and savory touch, couldn't be easier. Whenever I make them, I remember my dad's tip while picking out my anchovies: "The tiny ones taste better."

1 In a small bowl, combine the soy sauce, sesame oil, sugar, and pepper, stirring until the sugar dissolves. Set aside.

2 Set a medium nonstick frying pan over medium heat, and add 2 Tbsp of cooking oil. When the oil is hot, carefully add the garlic and allow it to cook for about 1 minute, or until the garlic turns golden.

3 Add the anchovies and stir-fry with a wooden spatula for about 3 minutes.

4 Add 2 Tbsp of water and cover the pan for about 2 minutes to allow the anchovies to steam.

5 Remove the lid and turn the heat to low. Add the soy sauce mixture and toss so the anchovies are coated, and allow to cook for another 2 minutes.

6 Transfer the anchovies to a serving dish, drizzle lightly with sesame oil, and toss to coat. Garnish with sesame seeds and serve. Store any leftovers in an airtight container in the refrigerator for up to 1 week.

SOUPS

STEWS

&

CHEONGGUKJANG JJIGAE (SOYBEAN PASTE STEW) SERVES 4 TO 5

3 cups [720 ml] Vegetable Anchovy Broth (page 158), or 3 cups [720 ml] water and 1 Tbsp anchovy sauce or fish sauce

1 small yellow onion, chopped

2 green onions, green and white parts separated and chopped

1 cup [150 g] napa cabbage kimchi, such as Mom & Dad's Kimchi (page 28), chopped

2 garlic cloves, minced

1 zucchini, sliced into ½ in [13 mm] thick quarters

¾ cup [185 g] cheonggukjang (soybean paste)

6 oz [170 g] firm tofu, cut into 1 in [2.5 cm] cubes

1 tsp gochugaru

Learning how to make this was really an ode to my mom and sister, Kathy. Apparently, my mother ate cheonggukjang jjigae a lot when she was pregnant with my sister, and we joke that this might be why Kathy often finds herself craving it out of nowhere! Yes, it has a strong smell, but this funky fermented stew is fantastic for your health due to the heaping amounts of probiotics, natural vitamins, and antioxidants in the soybean paste. Use sour aged kimchi to deepen the flavor of the broth, and add some mu (daikon radish) if you're a fan. Enjoy it with a bowl of rice and your favorite banchan.

1   In a medium pot over medium-high heat, combine the broth, yellow onion, green onion whites, kimchi, garlic, and zucchini. Bring the broth to a boil.

2   Turn the heat to medium-low and simmer for 15 minutes.

3   Add the cheonggukjang, breaking it up with a wooden spoon if necessary, and stir to incorporate.

4   Add the tofu and simmer for another 10 minutes, or until the tofu has softened.

5   Transfer the stew to serving bowls, and garnish with green onion greens and a sprinkle of gochugaru. Store any leftovers in an airtight container in the refrigerator for up to 5 days or freeze batches for up to 4 months, so you can have it through the cold winter!

DOENJANG JJIGAE (FERMENTED SOYBEAN PASTE STEW) SERVES 4 TO 5

Cooking oil

3 garlic cloves, minced

3 green onions, green and white parts separated and chopped

1 large Yukon gold potato, peeled and cut into 1 in [2.5 cm] cubes

1 large zucchini, cut into ½ in [13 mm] thick half-moon slices

1 green Korean chile, sliced

3 cups [720 ml] Vegetable Anchovy Broth (page 158), or 3 cups [720 ml] water and 1 Tbsp anchovy sauce or fish sauce

2 Tbsp doenjang

1 Tbsp gochujang

1 Tbsp toasted sesame oil

6 oz [170 g] silken tofu, cut into 1 in [2.5 cm] cubes

Gochugaru, for garnish

I'll admit that it took a while for me to appreciate doenjang jjigae (i.e., until I was an adult). This salty stew has a nice amount of funk. Once you've had it a few times, I bet you'll find yourself craving it on a cold day.

Cooking doenjang jjigae in my home involves some improvising: If I don't have an earthenware pot available, a Dutch oven works instead. Some folks opt for firm tofu, but I prefer silken, because it's a soft contrast to the rest of the contents of the stew and it takes on the surrounding flavors nicely. Also, some versions might include beef brisket, pork, or seafood, and sometimes potatoes, which add heartiness. However, even without the meat, it's deeply flavorful thanks to the vegetable anchovy broth. Doenjang jjigae is lovely alongside rice, kimchi, and other muchim (pages 46 to 63).

(cont.)

1   Set a Dutch oven over medium-high heat and lightly coat the
bottom of the pan with cooking oil. Allow the oil to heat for about
1 minute. Add the garlic and green onion whites and cook for
about 1 minute, tossing them in the hot oil with a wooden spatula.

2   Add the potato, stirring to combine, and cook for about 3 minutes.

3   Add the zucchini and chile and cook, stirring, for another 2 minutes.

4   Pour in the vegetable anchovy broth, and use a wooden spatula
to scrape up any brown bits that formed on the bottom of the pot.
Cover the pot and allow the liquid to come to a boil.

5   Once the broth comes to a boil, turn the heat to medium-low.
Add the doenjang, gochujang, and sesame oil, stirring well to
incorporate. Then add the tofu, cover the pot, and allow the stew
to simmer for 10 minutes.

6   Turn off the heat, stir in the green onion greens, and cover the pot.
Remove the pot from the heat and allow to sit for about 10 minutes
before serving.

7   Garnish with a dash or more of gochugaru to taste. Ladle and serve
in small individual bowls along with a bowl of hot steamed rice and
any other banchan you might have! Leftovers can be stored in an
airtight container in the fridge for up to 4 days.

CHICKEN & OYSTER MIYEOKGUK (CHICKEN & OYSTER SEAWEED SOUP) ^{SERVES 4}

1 oz [30 g] dried miyeok

Cooking oil

1 medium yellow onion, chopped or thinly sliced

4 cups [960 ml] chicken broth

8 oz [230 g] fresh oyster meat, chopped

Shredded cooked chicken breast (optional)

Toasted sesame oil, for garnish

2 green onions, green and white parts chopped

Miyeokguk serves several purposes in Korean culture, among them healing a mother after she gives birth and celebrating birthdays. Because it's full of nutrients and digestive aids, sometimes I'll order a big bowl of it on its own if I'm out late in K-town, instead of other late-night eats (don't laugh! I swear this is why I'm always in better shape than my friends the next morning!). I also always loved smelling this coming from the church kitchen; the adult congregation would make a large batch, and we'd all have it served in small Styrofoam cups along with our small lunch items after Sunday service.

Though I grew up having miyeokguk with beef, chicken is more common in my kitchen, and I usually have fresh chicken broth on hand to use as well. My dad likes adding chopped oysters, clams, or mussels to his recipe. I think of this rendition as a little meeting of the minds—some chicken, some oysters, lots of flavor.

(cont.)

1. In a large bowl of cold water, soak the miyeok for about 30 minutes. Rinse it two or three times and drain, squeezing out excess water. Chop the miyeok into bite-size pieces, and set aside.

2. Set a Dutch oven or stainless steel pot over medium-high heat and lightly coat the bottom of the pot with cooking oil. Add the yellow onion and cook for about 1 minute, then add the miyeok and cook, stirring, for 2 minutes.

3. Pour in the chicken broth, cover the pot, and bring the broth to a boil. Turn the heat to medium-low and simmer for another 20 to 25 minutes, or until the seaweed is just softened (don't let it go too long, or the texture will become pretty slimy).

4. Add the chopped oyster meat, and allow it to cook for 5 minutes, or until all the oyster meat has cooked through.

5. Stir in some chicken breast (if using).

6. Ladle the soup into serving bowls, garnish with a drizzle of sesame oil and a sprinkle of chopped green onions, and serve hot along with rice and more of your favorite banchan! Store in an airtight container in the refrigerator for up to 4 days.

KIMCHI JJIGAE (KIMCHI STEW) SERVES 4 TO 5

3 cups [720 ml]
Vegetable Anchovy
Broth (page 158)

1 cup [150 g] napa
cabbage kimchi, such
as Mom & Dad's Kimchi
(page 28), chopped

1 medium yellow onion,
chopped

8 oz [230 g] thick-sliced
pork belly, cut into ½ in
[13 mm] pieces

2 green onions, green
and white parts
separated and finely
chopped

½ Tbsp gochugaru

½ Tbsp gochujang

1 tsp soy sauce

1 tsp toasted sesame oil

6 oz [170 g] silken tofu,
cut into 1 in [2.5 cm]
cubes

I didn't fully appreciate kimchi jjigae until I went to college and smelled it coming from someone's nearby dorm room. The scent followed me; when my husband and I were living in our first apartment after we'd gotten married, there would always be someone cooking it down the hallway or upstairs. It smells and tastes of home, and it's always welcome!

Make sure that your kimchi is nice and sour—I'd say let it age at least two weeks in the fridge from when you first buy or make it. This recipe includes sliced pork, but feel free to substitute your preferred protein.

1. In a medium pot over medium-high heat, combine the broth, kimchi, yellow onion, pork belly, green onion whites, gochugaru, gochujang, soy sauce, and sesame oil. Cover the pot and bring the liquid to a boil. Turn the heat to medium-low and simmer, covered, for about 15 minutes.

2. Give the stew a good stir to combine everything, then add the tofu on top. Cover the pot again and cook for another 15 to 20 minutes, or until the pork is cooked through.

3. Remove the pot from the heat, add the green onion greens, and give it one last good stir.

4. Carefully ladle the stew into serving bowls, and serve hot. Leftovers can be stored in an airtight container in the fridge for up to 1 week.

HAEJANG GUK (HANGOVER SOUP) SERVES 4 TO 5

Cooking oil

3 green onions, green and white parts separated and finely chopped

3 garlic cloves, minced

1 or 2 large Yukon gold potatoes, peeled and chopped into 1 in [2.5 cm] cubes

Kosher salt

2 cups [480 ml] beef bone stock

1 Tbsp anchovy sauce or fish sauce

2 tsp gochugaru

1 tsp ground black pepper

1 lb [455 g] napa cabbage, chopped into 1 in [2.5 cm] pieces

2 Tbsp doenjang

2 Tbsp white miso paste

2 cups [360 g] cooked rice

Yup, the translation for haejang guk is, indeed, "hangover soup."

Though everyone seeks different ways to handle the aftermath of a hard night out, this soup can really handle the job. I personally am a fan of having this version of haejang guk, made with beef bone stock, especially Bibigo's bone broth. It tastes just like my parents' homemade stock—even *they* are fans of this store-bought option. The bone stock lends a great flavor, and the finished product will cure whatever ails ya!

Feel free to add whatever you'd like (again, your body will tell you what it needs after a big night!). Sometimes my haejang guk will have some kongnamul or some mushrooms depending on what's in the fridge, but this is the version I know my body likes and appreciates!

(cont.)

1 Set a Dutch oven or medium pot over medium-high heat and lightly coat the bottom of the pot with cooking oil. Allow the oil to heat for about 1 minute. Add the green onion whites and garlic and cook, stirring, for about 1 minute.

2 Add the potatoes, stirring to combine, and cook for about 2 minutes. Season with a generous pinch of salt.

3 Add the beef stock and 2 cups [480 ml] of water along with the anchovy sauce, gochugaru, and pepper. Stir to combine, cover the pot, and bring the liquid to a boil.

4 Turn the heat to medium-low and add the napa cabbage. Cover the pot again and simmer for about 15 minutes or until the cabbage is tender and wilted.

5 Meanwhile, in a small bowl, combine the doenjang and miso paste with a small amount of the hot broth from the pot, whisking with a fork until all the lumps are gone.

6 Turn the heat to low and add the doenjang mixture to the pot, stirring to combine. Cover the pot and let it continue to simmer for 5 to 10 minutes, or until the potatoes are fully cooked.

7 Ladle the soup into bowls and add a scoop of rice, ⅓ to ¼ cup [80 to 100 g], to each bowl. Garnish with green onion greens. Serve with a big glass of water to drive that hangover away! Leftover soup can be stored in an airtight container in the fridge for up to 4 days.

HAEMUL SUNDUBU JJIGAE (SPICY TOFU STEW WITH SEAFOOD) SERVES 2 TO 4

Cooking oil

4 oz [115 g] thick-cut pork belly slices, cut into ½ in [13 mm] pieces

1 small yellow onion, chopped

1 cup [150 g] napa cabbage kimchi, such as Mom & Dad's Kimchi (page 28), chopped

3 shiitake mushrooms, stems removed, cut into ½ in [13 mm] slices

1 Tbsp gochugaru

1 tsp toasted sesame oil

1 cup [240 ml] Vegetable Anchovy Broth (page 158)

6 oz [170 g] silken tofu

5 to 7 fresh mussels, scrubbed and debearded

1 egg

2 green onions, green and white parts chopped

Garlic Anchovy Oil (page 160; optional), for garnish

My favorite version of sundubu jjigae (spicy tofu stew) is haemul sundubu jjigae (with seafood). Though many have shrimp with theirs, due to my father's allergy, this version is usually the one that makes it onto my kitchen table. I love the simplicity of it, with the added flavors of some mussels and shiitake mushrooms. It's delicious as part of a KBBQ table with rice, meat, and vegetables!

Serve this in small earthenware pots or bowls to retain the heat, but if they are unavailable, make it in a Dutch oven or trusty pot and serve in small bowls.

(cont.)

1. Set a Dutch oven or large pot over medium-high heat and lightly coat the bottom of the pot with cooking oil. Allow the oil to heat for about 1 minute. Add the pork belly and yellow onion and cook, stirring with a wooden spatula, for about 4 minutes, or until the pork is browned.

2. Add the kimchi, mushrooms, gochugaru, and sesame oil and continue cooking for 2 to 3 minutes, stirring continuously until the kimchi is softened.

3. Pour in the vegetable anchovy broth, cover the pot, and bring the liquid to a boil. Turn the heat to medium-low and simmer for about 10 minutes.

4. Turn the heat to low. Add the tofu however you prefer: Cut it into small pieces, or use a spoon to roughly cut it up—if using a soft tofu cylinder tube, squeeze it right into the pot.

5. Add the mussels, cover the pot, and cook for about 3 minutes, or until the mussels open. Discard any mussels that do not open.

6. Crack the egg right into the stew and let everything cook, uncovered, for another 1 to 2 minutes (the egg will continue cooking in the hot broth after you turn off the heat). You can stir in the egg to enrich the broth, or allow it to float on top until it's poached.

7. Ladle the soup into bowls, garnish with the chopped green onions and a drizzle of garlic anchovy oil (if using), and serve with hot rice. Leftovers can be stored in an airtight container in the refrigerator for up to 3 days.

BUCHIMG

(Pancakes

AE

PAJEON (GREEN ONION PANCAKE)

SERVES 4 TO 5 (MAKES 1 LARGE PANCAKE)

DIPPING SAUCE

¼ cup [60 ml] toasted sesame oil

3 Tbsp soy sauce

1 Tbsp rice wine vinegar or white vinegar

1 Tbsp honey or sugar

1 green onion, green and white parts finely chopped

1 garlic clove, minced

Kosher salt

Ground black pepper

¼ tsp toasted sesame seeds (optional)

Gochugaru, for garnish (optional)

PANCAKE

1 cup [140 g] all-purpose flour

1 Tbsp cornstarch

1 Tbsp doenjang

1 tsp toasted sesame oil

1 tsp kosher salt, plus more as needed

1 cup [240 ml] cold water

8 to 10 green onion greens cut about 3 in [7.5 cm] long

¼ cup [60 ml] cooking oil

Ground black pepper

I have come to learn that the scent of sizzling onions means that a delicious *something* is on the horizon. For me, pajeon (or really, any jeon/pancake) is one of those transportive dishes that takes me back to eating at gatherings with my extended family. Not only is it incredibly easy to make (mainly flour, water, and green onions), but my goodness, the aroma is powerful! It's a staple for the Chuseok holiday, the Korean mid-autumn festival, but really, it's fit for any occasion.

There are different ways to prepare jeon: You can pre-fry your green onions if you want to be ultra-traditionalist, or not; I promise the jeon police won't come for you! I also sometimes add a small spoonful of doenjang or white miso paste to the batter to give it just a little extra flavor and saltiness.

They say the key to extra crispy jeon is to cook it in lots of oil; I leave it to your discretion to use more than my recommended amount!

(cont.)

MAKE THE DIPPING SAUCE:

1 In a small bowl, combine the sesame oil, soy sauce, vinegar, honey, green onion, garlic, and a pinch each of salt and pepper, and whisk together with a fork. Add the sesame seeds (if using) and/or a pinch of gochugaru for a good kick (if using).

MAKE THE PANCAKE:

1 In a large bowl, combine the flour, cornstarch, doenjang, sesame oil, salt, and the cold water. Whisk together well, just until the batter is smooth. Stir in the green onions.

2 Set a nonstick 9 in [23 cm] frying pan over medium heat and pour in the cooking oil. Let the oil heat for about 1 minute, or until it is shimmering.

3 Carefully ladle in all of the green onion batter (being wary of possible splashing). Cook the pancake for 3 to 4 minutes on each side, or until both sides are crispy and golden brown. To flip, use a large spatula or two small ones.

4 Transfer the pancake to a plate, season it with salt and pepper, and cut it into wedges. Serve hot! If there are leftovers, let cool, then layer with parchment paper, place in an airtight container or plastic storage bag, and refrigerate for up to 4 days or freeze for up to 2 months. Reheat defrosted wedges on both sides in a lightly oiled frying pan over medium heat.

HOBAKJEON (ZUCCHINI PANCAKE)

SERVES 4 TO 5 (MAKES 1 LARGE PANCAKE)

1 cup [140 g] all-purpose flour

1 Tbsp cornstarch

1 tsp toasted sesame oil

1 tsp kosher salt, plus more as needed

¼ tsp ground black pepper, plus more as needed

½ cup [120 ml] cold water

1 medium zucchini, cut into matchsticks

¼ cup [60 ml] cooking oil

Hobakjeon is as simple as Pajeon (page 106) to make, and very tasty. The moisture from the zucchini makes for a tender pancake with crispy edges. It's one of my favorite banchan to have in any season not just because of its light flavor, but for its heartiness too.

Very often, you'll see hobakjeon made as dredged and fried zucchini discs, which is a total time saver and still very traditional. However, I highly recommend cooking your hobakjeon as pancakes with zucchini matchsticks. You won't be able to eat just one!

(cont.)

1   In a large bowl, combine the flour, cornstarch, sesame oil, salt, and pepper with the cold water. Whisk together well, just until the batter is smooth. Stir in the zucchini.

2   Set a nonstick 9 in [23 cm] frying pan over medium heat and pour in the cooking oil. Let the oil heat for about 1 minute, or until the oil is shimmering.

3   Carefully ladle in all of the batter (being wary of possible splashing). Cook the pancake for 3 to 5 minutes on each side, or until both sides are crispy and golden brown.

4   Transfer the pancake to a plate, season it with salt and pepper, and cut it into wedges. Serve hot! If there are leftovers, let cool, then layer with parchment paper, place in an airtight container or plastic storage bag, and refrigerate for up to 3 days or freeze for up to 2 months. Reheat defrosted wedges on both sides in a lightly oiled frying pan over medium heat.

KIMCHIJEON (KIMCHI PANCAKE)

SERVES 4 TO 5 (MAKES 1 LARGE PANCAKE)

½ cup [70 g] all-purpose flour

1 Tbsp cornstarch

1 cup [150 g] napa cabbage kimchi with brine, such as Mom & Dad's Kimchi (page 28), cut into 1 in [2.5 cm] pieces

1 green onion, green and white parts chopped

½ tsp ground black pepper

½ cup [120 ml] cold water

¼ cup [60 ml] cooking oil

Kosher salt

There is nothing quite like the comfort of a crisp kimchijeon and a bowl of gomtang (beef bone soup). And, like most banchan, this recipe is quick to make, classic, and absolutely delicious!

Don't skip including that spicy kimchi brine when mixing in your kimchi. That stuff is liquid gold! For those seeking a little more heat than just what their kimchi provides: Feel free to add a bit of gochujang or gochugaru flakes to the batter too.

1   In a large bowl, combine the flour, cornstarch, kimchi (and brine!), green onion, and pepper with the cold water. Whisk together well with a fork, just until the batter is smooth.

2   Set a nonstick 9 in [23 cm] frying pan over medium heat and pour in the oil. Let the oil heat for about 1 minute, or until it is shimmering.

3   Carefully ladle in all of the batter (being wary of possible splashing). Cook the pancake for 3 to 4 minutes on each side, until the edges are crispy and both sides are golden brown.

4   Transfer the pancake to a plate, season with salt to taste, cut into wedges, and serve hot! If there are leftovers, let cool, then layer with parchment paper, place in an airtight container or plastic storage bag, and refrigerate for up to 3 days or freeze for up to 1 month. Reheat defrosted wedges on both sides in a lightly oiled frying pan over medium heat.

HAEMUL PAJEON (SEAFOOD PANCAKE) SERVES 4 TO 5 (MAKES 1 LARGE PANCAKE)

1 cup [140 g] all-purpose flour

1 egg

1 Tbsp cornstarch

1 Tbsp doenjang

1 tsp toasted sesame oil

1 tsp kosher salt, plus more as needed

½ tsp ground black pepper, plus more as needed

¼ cup [60 ml] cooking oil

5 oz [140 g] fresh seafood of choice (such as shrimp, mussels, clams, squid—or a mixture), cleaned and cut into ½ in [13 mm] pieces

8 green onion greens, cut about 3 in [7.5 cm] long

Whenever I go to a Korean restaurant with my friends or family, someone will, without fail, get an order of haemul pajeon to share with the table. When I first started making haemul pajeon at home, I quickly realized that it takes a bit more skill to make than other jeon. With so much water from the seafood and green onions in the batter, it can be a little tricky to flip. The results might not be pretty, but they're still quite tasty!

I've since mastered the haemul pajeon flip, and you can too; all it takes is a bit of practice and confidence. Sometimes, using two spatulas can help if the pancake is too heavy. And it's definitely worth it: A treat to have in a restaurant, haemul pajeon is even more special when served at home.

(cont.)

1 In a large bowl, combine the flour, egg, cornstarch, doenjang, sesame oil, salt, and pepper with 1 cup [240 ml] of water. Whisk together well, just until the batter is smooth.

2 Set a nonstick 9 in [23 cm] frying pan over medium heat and pour in the cooking oil. Let the oil heat for about 1 minute, or until it is shimmering.

3 Carefully ladle in half of the batter (being wary of possible splashing). Scatter the seafood on the surface and place the green onion greens in an even layer on top, then ladle the remaining batter on top.

4 Cook the pancake for about 5 minutes, or until the bottom is crispy and browned. If you find the pancake is browning too fast, lower the heat.

5 Using a large spatula (or two if the pancake needs the extra support!), carefully flip the pancake.

6 Allow the pancake to cook for another 3 minutes, or until the second side is crispy and the seafood is cooked through.

7 Transfer the pancake to a plate, season with salt and pepper, cut it into wedges, and serve hot! This is best eaten after it's made; the seafood can become tough and chewy if reheated.

KOGIJEON (MEAT PANCAKE)

SERVES 4 TO 5 (MAKES ABOUT 20 PANCAKES, DEPENDING ON HOW BIG YOUR SLICES OF BEEF ARE)

1 lb [455 g] thinly sliced rib eye

Kosher salt

Ground black pepper

½ cup [70 g] all-purpose flour

3 extra-large eggs

2 tsp toasted sesame oil

¼ cup [60 ml] cooking oil

1 red chile, sliced, for garnish (optional)

Making kogijeon was always a family effort in my house. Whenever we had guests coming over or a special occasion, all hands were on deck to dredge and dip the beef, then carefully hand it off to whoever was on griddle duty to fry the pieces. Thus, of all jeon, I feel most nostalgic toward kogijeon.

Though not a traditional pancake, the meat is egg-battered and pan-fried and served with rice. You can usually buy the thin rib eye presliced from your local Asian supermarket, all ready to go. However, if you're slicing the meat on your own, freezing it for about 30 minutes beforehand can help make it easier to slice. If you'd like to go for a leaner cut of beef, a thinly cut sirloin also works.

(cont.)

1   Season the beef with a pinch each of salt and pepper.

2   In a medium bowl, mix the flour with 1 tsp of salt.

3   In a separate medium bowl, beat the eggs well with 1 tsp of the sesame oil, 1 tsp of salt, ½ tsp of pepper, and a splash of water.

4   In a large nonstick frying pan over medium heat, combine the cooking oil and the remaining 1 tsp of sesame oil and let heat for about 1 minute.

5   While the oil heats, dredge a slice of beef in the seasoned flour, then carefully dip the slice in the egg mixture until completely coated. When the oil is shimmering, carefully place the slice flat in the oil. Repeat with a few more slices of beef, being mindful not to crowd the pan.

6   Cook the beef for 1 to 2 minutes on each side, or until the egg on the outside is completely cooked and the meat appears to be browned. Transfer to a plate lined with paper towels, then prepare more pieces of beef. Repeat until all of the slices are cooked. If the pan becomes dry, carefully wipe out any bits of fried egg and then pour in more oil.

7   Season the kogijeon slices with a pinch each of salt and pepper, garnish with the red chile (if using), and serve. If there are leftovers, let cool, then layer with parchment paper, place in an airtight container or plastic storage bag, and refrigerate for up to 3 days or freeze for up to 1 month. Reheat defrosted wedges on both sides in a lightly oiled frying pan over medium heat.

DONGTAEJEON (POLLOCK PANCAKE)

SERVES 5 TO 6 (MAKES 10 TO 12 SMALL PANCAKES)

1 lb [455 g] frozen
pollock fillets

Kosher salt

Ground black pepper

1 cup [140 g] all-purpose
flour

2 eggs

2 tsp toasted sesame oil

¼ cup [60 ml] cooking oil

Toasted sesame seeds,
for garnish (optional)

1 red chile, sliced, for
garnish (optional)

A few years ago, Eric and I spent a couple weeks in Hawai'i, and while there, Eric found every reason to include his favorite, fish jeon, with our meals. Like, drag-me-out-of-bed-early-in-the-morning-to-get-it-with-breakfast favorite.

You can use cod for this, but my family are big fans of pollock. It's a tasty but lean whitefish, inexpensive, and very popular in Korean cooking. After a little time preparing the fish, jeon magic is made by dredging, frying, and (our favorite part) eating!

(cont.)

1 Thaw the frozen fish in a bowl with 2 cups [480 ml] of water mixed with ½ Tbsp of salt. Once the fillets are defrosted and tender, pat them dry with paper towels.

2 With a sharp knife, slice the fish into 2 in [5 cm] square pieces (check for and remove any bones). Season the pieces on both sides with salt and pepper and set aside on paper towels.

3 In a medium bowl, combine the flour with 1 tsp of salt and ½ tsp of pepper.

4 In a separate medium bowl, beat the eggs well with 1 tsp of the sesame oil, a few generous pinches of salt and pepper, and a splash of cold water.

5 In a large nonstick frying pan over medium heat, combine the cooking oil and the remaining 1 tsp of sesame oil and let heat for about 1 minute.

6 While the oil heats, dredge a pollock slice in the seasoned flour, then carefully dip the it in the egg mixture until completely coated. When the oil is shimmering, carefully place the slice in the oil. Repeat with a few more pollock slices, being mindful not to crowd the pan.

7 Cook the slices for 1 to 2 minutes on each side, or until the egg coating is completely cooked on the outside and the pollock is cooked white. Transfer each piece to a plate lined with paper towels, then prepare more fillets. Repeat until all of the pieces are cooked. If the pan becomes dry, carefully wipe out any bits of fried egg and then pour in more oil.

8 While they're still hot, season the fillets with a pinch each of salt and pepper, garnish with sesame seeds and/or the red chile (if using), and serve hot. If there are leftovers, let cool, then layer with parchment paper, place in an airtight container or plastic storage bag, and refrigerate for up to 2 days or freeze for up to 1 month. Reheat defrosted wedges on both sides in a lightly oiled frying pan over medium heat.

BINDAETTEOK (MUNG BEAN PANCAKE)

SERVES 3 (MAKES 6 SMALL PANCAKES)

BINDAETTEOK

2 cups [400 g] dried and peeled yellow mung beans (see Note)

1 egg

½ cup [120 ml] cold water

2 Tbsp kimchi brine

2 Tbsp soy sauce

1 tsp anchovy sauce

1 Tbsp toasted sesame oil

Kosher salt

1 cup [150 g] aged napa cabbage kimchi, such as Mom & Dad's Kimchi (page 28), chopped

¼ cup [40 g] sweet rice flour

3 green onions, green and white parts roughly chopped

Cooking oil

DIPPING SAUCE

2 Tbsp toasted sesame oil

2 Tbsp soy sauce

1 Tbsp white vinegar

1 tsp honey

1 green onion, green and white parts finely chopped

½ tsp ground black pepper

note: Buy mung beans pre-peeled at the supermarket or online.

In my family, picking a favorite between my mother or my aunt's bindaetteok was always a toss-up. Truly, though, we were always just happy to be on the receiving end of either!

Some might scoff at my go-to recipe since it strays a bit from a traditional bindaetteok, but it's made primarily with pantry staples, and you can't beat that. Some folks will add meat or more spices to theirs—everyone can give it their own touch! My method calls for soaking the hulled mung beans and grinding them, because I like a bit of texture. But you can make this with mung bean flour instead—just substitute the mung beans and rice flour with 1½ cups [120 g] mung bean flour. Good food takes time, so really, think of it as something to look forward to and a delicious labor of love!

(cont.)

MAKE THE BINDAETTEOK:

1 Rinse the mung beans under cold water, drain, then transfer to a large bowl. Add cold water to cover by 1 in [2.5 cm]. Soak the mung beans for at least 6 hours and up to 24 hours (don't go past 24 hours, or else they'll be too mushy).

2 Drain the mung beans, and place them in a blender or food processor. Add the egg, water, kimchi brine, soy sauce, anchovy sauce, sesame oil, and a generous pinch of salt. Blend until it is coarsely puréed (don't overdo it!).

3 In a large mixing bowl, combine the kimchi, rice flour, and green onion. Gradually add the mung bean mixture, using a rubber spatula to mix them together.

4 Set a large nonstick frying pan over medium-high heat and lightly coat the bottom of the pan with cooking oil. Allow the oil to heat for about 1 minute, or until the oil is shimmering. Ladle about 1 cup [240 ml] of batter onto the pan and cook the pancake for 3 minutes on each side, or until crisp and browned. Transfer the pancake to a plate lined with paper towels, and repeat with the remaining batter.

MAKE THE DIPPING SAUCE AND SERVE:

1 In a small bowl, combine the sesame oil, soy sauce, vinegar, honey, green onion, and pepper.

2 Serve the bindaetteok hot with the dipping sauce on the side. If there are leftovers, let cool, then layer with parchment paper, place in an airtight container or plastic storage bag, and refrigerate for up to 3 days or freeze for up to 1 month. Reheat defrosted bindaetteok on both sides in a lightly oiled frying pan over medium heat.

(part 2) Banchan

om My Kitchen

COLD
BANCHA

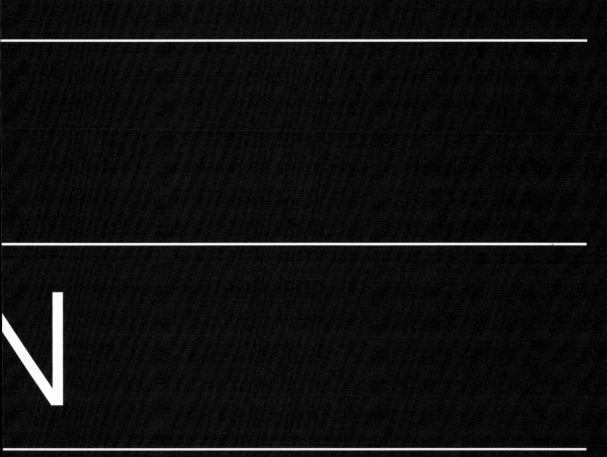

ASIAN PEAR & GREEN ONION KIMCHI SERVES 4 TO 5

2 Asian pears, peeled and chopped into 1 in [2.5 cm] cubes

Kosher salt

4 green onions, thinly sliced lengthwise

2 garlic cloves, minced

1 tsp grated peeled fresh ginger

1 carrot, cut into matchsticks

1 Tbsp toasted sesame oil

1 Tbsp sugar

1 Tbsp gochugaru

2 tsp soy sauce

Toasted sesame seeds, for garnish (optional)

My husband is THAT person: the one who completely embraces Asian pear season by the huge boxful. He'd eat one every day if he could! This recipe came to me in an effort to utilize a plethora of Asian pears and an abundant supply of green onions on sale at H Mart. It reminds me of a sweet and savory version of Kkakdugi (page 38), using pears in place of daikon. If Asian pears aren't available to you, a few Bosc pears will also work well.

1   In a large mixing bowl, combine the pears with a generous dousing of salt, tossing to coat. Let the pears sit for about 30 minutes.

2   Rinse and drain the pears well, patting them dry with paper towels, and return them to the bowl.

3   Meanwhile, in a small bowl, soak the green onions in 2 cups [480 ml] of cold water mixed with a dash of salt, for 10 minutes.

4   Drain the green onions, pat dry with paper towels, and add them to the bowl with the pears.

5   To the pears and green onions, add the garlic, ginger, carrot, sesame oil, sugar, gochugaru, and soy sauce. With gloved hands, mix everything together well.

6   Transfer the pears and green onions into an airtight glass jar and seal the lid. Let sit at room temperature for 12 hours, then serve or store in the refrigerator for up to 1 week. Garnish with sesame seeds (if using), before serving.

CREAMY KIMCHI BACON DIP SERVES 5 TO 6

5 oz [140 g] napa cabbage kimchi, such as Mom & Dad's Kimchi (page 28)

4 strips of bacon, cooked and broken into bits

½ cup [120 g] sour cream or 2 percent Greek yogurt

½ cup [120 g] mayonnaise

1 tsp white vinegar

1 tsp honey or agave nectar

½ tsp onion powder

½ tsp garlic powder

½ tsp smoked paprika

¼ tsp ground cumin

¼ tsp mustard powder

2 Tbsp chopped fresh chives or green onions

Kosher salt

Ground black pepper

Kimchi and bacon go together like old friends. This dip has a lot of layered flavor, thanks to the warm spices, the bright bite of kimchi, and the richness from the dairy and mayonnaise. You can also make a fantastic vegan version of this dip with vegan-friendly kimchi, yogurt, and mayo, and plant-based bacon. (Of course, you can also skip the bacon altogether, though I personally find that less fun. But to each their own!) Whatever you choose, it will no doubt disappear very quickly from your appetizer tray. This is the version that makes my taste buds sing. I hope it will do the same for you!

1   In a food processor, combine the kimchi, bacon, sour cream, mayonnaise, vinegar, honey, onion powder, garlic powder, smoked paprika, cumin, mustard powder, chives, and a dash each of salt and pepper.

2   Blitz the mixture until it reaches as smooth a texture as possible.

3   Transfer the mixture to a serving bowl and serve with crudités or chips. Store in an airtight container in the refrigerator for up to 3 days.

STRAWBERRY CITRUS GEOTJEORI SERVES 4

1 lb [455 g] chopped strawberries

3 Persian or Kirby cucumbers, sliced

1 Tbsp kosher salt

2½ Tbsp gochugaru

1 Tbsp anchovy sauce or kelp powder (for a vegan version)

½ Tbsp sugar

½ Tbsp soy sauce

1 Tbsp toasted sesame oil

2 tsp rice vinegar

½ Tbsp grated peeled fresh ginger

2 garlic cloves, minced

Zest and juice of 1 lime, plus more (optional) for garnish

Zest and juice of 1 orange, plus more (optional) for garnish

2 green onions, green and white parts finely chopped

1 tsp ground black pepper

Toasted sesame seeds, for garnish

This recipe was created after I picked pounds upon pounds of strawberries one summer and just did not want to turn on the stove or oven to make jam or pie (no joke!). This wonderful fresh kimchi goes especially well with a summer barbecue spread or a good fried chicken meal. My sister is a fan of sipping on the leftover juice!

If making the vegan version, mix the kelp powder well with your liquids before mixing them with the strawberries and cucumbers.

(cont.)

1 In a medium bowl, combine the strawberries, cucumbers, and salt. Let sit for about 1 hour, or at least 30 minutes.

2 Strain out any excess liquid into a small bowl and set aside. Give the cucumbers and strawberries a quick rinse under cold water, drain fully, and return them to the bowl.

3 In a separate small bowl, combine the gochugaru, anchovy sauce, sugar, soy sauce, sesame oil, vinegar, ginger, garlic, citrus zests and juices, green onions, pepper, and a spoonful of the strawberry-cucumber liquid, stirring until the sugar dissolves.

4 Gradually pour the sauce over the cucumbers and strawberries, and with gloved hands to protect your skin, mix together well.

5 Garnish with sesame seeds and a bit of additional fresh citrus zest (if using). Serve immediately! Leftovers can be stored in an airtight container in the fridge for up to 2 days, but note that the texture will become softer.

KIMBAP MAKES 4 ROLLS (64 PIECES)

8 oz [230 g] thinly sliced
rib eye

2 Tbsp toasted sesame
oil

1 Tbsp sugar

2 tsp soy sauce

4 cups [750 g] cooked
short-grain white sushi
rice, still warm

1½ tsp kosher salt, plus
more as needed

4 sheets roasted
seaweed, each about
7½ by 8 in [19 by 20 cm]

1 cucumber, cut into
lengthwise strips

1 carrot, cut into
matchsticks

2 eggs, cooked into an
omelette and cut into
long thin strips

4 pieces yellow radish,
cut thinly into 8 in
[20 cm] strips

1 cup [30 g] fresh
spinach, blanched

Think of kimbap as the party house that banchan are always invited to. So many banchan can be repurposed in kimbap with delicious results.

Growing up, I often heard people call kimbap "Korean-style sushi" and it always made my eyes roll because there is no raw fish in kimbap! Though of course they are both seaweed rolls, kimbap has an identity all its own. Whether packed with vegetables, ham or spam, or purple or white rice, every Korean and Korean American family has their own appetizing way of making kimbap.

The first time I made kimbap on my own was an epic fail, even though I'd done it many times with my family! You name it, it happened: the seaweed tore easily; the rice was over-oiled for one roll and dried out for the next; after slicing the rolls they looked like deflated toy car tires. However, that's part of the joy of the homemade kimbap experience: practicing until those delicious mistakes become beautiful results.

You can usually find a lot of premade or precut vegetables in Asian supermarkets that are the perfect size for kimbap rolls. I'm personally a big fan of precut yellow radish (pickled daikon). If you're planning to include eggs in your kimbap, cook them into an omelette first and cut them into strips so they're ready to go in with everything else. Use a small, hand-rolling bamboo mat to help form those packed seaweed rolls and a good, trusty knife to cut the rolls as neatly as possible.

Kimbap will dry out in the fridge and won't be as tender if stored overnight, but if you want to revive dried day-old kimbap, dip it in beaten eggs like French toast, and fry on both sides for 30 seconds!

(cont.)

1. In a medium bowl, combine the rib eye, 1 Tbsp of the sesame oil, the sugar, and the soy sauce, tossing until the rib eye is fully coated. (It's best done with a gloved hand.)

2. In a large skillet over medium-high heat, cook the meat for 3 to 5 minutes, or until the meat is browned and cooked through. Set aside on a plate to cool.

3. In a large bowl, season the cooked rice (while it's still warm) with the salt and the remaining 1 Tbsp of sesame oil. Set aside.

4. Place a sheet of seaweed on a bamboo rolling mat with the shiny side down.

5. Carefully spread about 1 cup of rice over about two-thirds of the surface of the seaweed, leaving about 2 in [5 cm] at the top of the sheet uncovered.

6. Place a thin strip of rib eye running down the length of the rice toward the bottom, followed by a strip of cucumber, carrots, egg, yellow radish, and spinach. Lightly salt the vegetables and egg for a little extra flavor, if you want.

7. Use both hands and the bamboo mat to firmly but carefully roll the bottom of the seaweed sheet over the fillings, and continue rolling until the seaweed is completely rolled up. Gently wet your fingertip with a little water and moisten the inside of the bare flap of seaweed to ensure it sticks to the roll. Hold the roll tightly in the mat for about 10 seconds to help secure.

8. Transfer the roll to a cutting board and carefully slice it into ½ in [13 mm] pieces.

9. Repeat with the remaining ingredients.

10. Serve immediately, or pack it up to take to a picnic and eat at room temperature on the same day.

KIMCHI AVOCADO NIGIRI SERVES 4 TO 5

2 cups [400 g] short-grain white sushi rice

1 Tbsp sugar

1 Tbsp white vinegar

1 cup [150 g] napa cabbage kimchi, such as Mom & Dad's Kimchi (page 28), finely chopped and excess liquid squeezed out

1 avocado, thinly sliced

Toasted sesame seeds, for garnish

When my dad wants to celebrate something, he happily prepares a sushi and sashimi platter. Unfortunately, due to my raw fish allergy, I'm not able to indulge, so this is what he came up with to ensure I'd have something to eat. He's quite proud of it, and I'm definitely more than happy to eat it.

Of course I had to edit his recipe a bit, but there are some things he insists on emphasizing to those preparing this at home: Chef's choice applies when seasoning your nigiri—use more sugar or vinegar depending on how you like it—and it's very important to squeeze the gukmool (kimchi brine) out of the kimchi so it doesn't make your rice too watery.

This recipe inspired him to call me four times in a row to confirm he'd given me the exact right measurements; on one of the calls he scolded me for letting out delighted giggles over how cute it was to read his directions to make a "dimple" in the ball of rice. Have at it and enjoy!

(cont.)

1   **If cooking the rice in a rice cooker:** Rinse and drain the rice twice, until the water runs clear. Place the rice and water to the line indicated for "sushi rice" in the rice cooker, and let soak for 30 minutes. Steam the rice according to the cooker's instructions.

   If cooking the rice on the stovetop: Rinse and drain the rice until the water runs clear. Place the rice and 2½ cups [600 ml] of water in a medium pot, and let soak for 30 minutes. Place the lid on the pot, set the pot over high heat, and bring it to a boil. Immediately turn the heat to low and simmer the rice for about 30 minutes. Turn off the heat, and let rest for 15 minutes. Carefully remove the lid to release the steam.

2   While the rice is still warm, add the sugar and vinegar and combine using a rice paddle or large spoon.

3   With your hands, form a small ball (about 2 in [5 cm] wide) of seasoned rice, then make a small dimple in the center of the ball. Fill the dimple with a small amount of the kimchi. Gently squeeze the rice to secure the kimchi in the dimple, and smooth out the shape of the rice ball. Transfer it to a cold plate.

4   Top each ball with a slice of avocado, garnish with sesame seeds, and serve.

KIMCHI POTATO SALAD SERVES 6 TO 8

3 lb [1.4 kg] Yukon gold potatoes, peeled and chopped into 1 in [2.5 cm] pieces

Kosher salt

1 cup [150 g] napa cabbage kimchi, such as Mom & Dad's Kimchi (page 28), finely chopped

2 celery stalks, diced

¼ cup fresh chives or green onions, chopped, plus more for garnish

½ cup [120 g] mayonnaise

½ cup [120 g] sour cream or Greek yogurt

1½ Tbsp Dijon mustard

1 tsp red wine vinegar

½ tsp honey

1 tsp onion powder

½ tsp smoked paprika

½ tsp ground black pepper

Gochugaru, for garnish (optional)

Among the banchan at a KBBQ restaurant, you might see a small plate of macaroni or potato salad. Though not a traditional Korean dish, potato salad appeals to many, and when a scoop appears in a tiny banchan dish, it's irresistible. It will often have a bit of sweetness and creaminess to it, and sometimes a cold crunch from shredded cucumbers, corn, or carrots. I decided to combine the best of all worlds in this recipe, which features the saltiness and spiciness of kimchi and comfort of a soft American potato salad.

I kid you not, the first time I made this recipe, I made a full three pounds of it and brought it over to my parents' house in a giant Tupperware container for them to try, expecting it to be part of their meals for the next several days. I still remember my mom's gleeful phone call the *next day*, giggling as she told me, "Oh, I ate ALL of your potato salad. It was SO del-ish-us!" My mom continues to impress me by packing away large amounts of food in her tiny body. Such a talent.

You can cut down how much you make of this, but I *always* want leftovers to share and have for days! Serve this at a potluck, and I bet you folks will eagerly come back for seconds. Or, if you are like my mom, you will finish it all in one night. As my dear childhood crush, Academy Award–winner (!!!) Ke Huy Quan, said as Short Round in *Indiana Jones and the Temple of Doom*, "Okey dokey, Dr. Jones. Hold on to your potatoes!"

(cont.)

1   Put the potatoes in a large pot and sprinkle with 1 Tbsp of salt. Fill the pot with enough water to cover the potatoes by 1 in [2.5 cm]. Set the pot over high heat and bring the water to a boil, then lower the heat to maintain a simmer for 15 minutes, or until the potatoes are fork-tender. Drain the potatoes and place them in a large mixing bowl. Set aside.

2   In a medium bowl, combine the kimchi, celery, chives, mayonnaise, sour cream, mustard, vinegar, honey, onion powder, paprika, 1 tsp of salt, and the pepper, mixing until fully combined.

3   While the potatoes are still warm, add the kimchi mixture to the potatoes and use a large spoon, fork, or rubber spatula to thoroughly combine.

4   Once the potato salad has completely cooled, cover the bowl with plastic wrap or transfer to a storage container with an airtight lid, and refrigerate for at least 2 hours or overnight to allow all the flavors to meld together.

5   Garnish with more chives and gochugaru (if using) for a little extra spiciness, and serve. Store leftovers in an airtight container in the refrigerator for up to 5 days.

SESAME EGG SALAD SERVES 4

6 hard-boiled eggs, cooled, peeled, and roughly chopped

1 small shallot, minced

2 celery stalks, finely chopped

2 Tbsp Dijon mustard

2 Tbsp Kewpie mayonnaise

1 Tbsp toasted sesame oil

½ Tbsp white vinegar

2 tsp truffle oil

2 tsp agave nectar or honey

2 Tbsp fresh chives, finely chopped

1 tsp smoked paprika

1 Tbsp toasted sesame seeds, for garnish

Roasted seaweed, thinly sliced, for garnish

Black truffle salt, for garnish

I still remember the first time I had egg salad. It was served along with lunch in the extended-day preschool program I was in. Though it sometimes gets a bad rap, egg salad is a classic. This is the version I make often to have in our house to accompany any meal of the day (including breakfast)! It's a little less creamy than that first one I tried and has plenty of toastiness and flavor. Serve with a bowl of rice and your preferred banchan dishes.

1   In a medium bowl, combine the eggs, shallot, celery, mustard, mayonnaise, sesame oil, vinegar, truffle oil, agave nectar, chives, and smoked paprika, mixing well to combine.

2   Garnish with the sesame seeds, some bits of roasted seaweed, and a sprinkling of black truffle salt. Serve immediately or cover and chill for 3 hours before serving. Store leftovers in an airtight container for up to 2 days.

SESAME TUNA SALAD
SERVES 4 TO 5

10 oz [280 g] water-packed white-meat tuna, drained

¼ cup [60 g] mayonnaise

2 Tbsp Dijon mustard

2 celery stalks, finely chopped

1 Tbsp toasted sesame oil

1 tsp onion powder

1 tsp furikake, plus more for garnish

1 tsp kosher salt, plus more as needed

½ tsp ground black pepper

½ tsp smoked paprika

½ tsp agave nectar or honey

Fresh lemon juice (optional)

Toasted sesame seeds, for garnish

For a short time when I was in the first grade, my mom used to pack a can of tuna in my lunch. Not long after, a small dish of plain canned tuna fish appeared on our dinner table to go along with our rice, vegetables, and gim. I'm not sure where her preference evolved from, but as I got older, I realized how just a simple can of tuna can serve as the basis for different kinds of meals and be handy for making a lot from a little!

I am fan of good water-packed tuna, and for excellent taste and tenderness, I recommend the Korean canned tuna brand Dongwon. Try it for your tuna salad needs, in kimbap, or whenever you're craving a deopbap—a bowl of smothered rice with tuna. This is my go-to tuna salad recipe when I want a little lightness still with plenty of flavor!

1 In a medium bowl, add the tuna fish and break it up lightly with a fork.

2 To the bowl, add the mayonnaise, mustard, celery, sesame oil, onion powder, furikake, salt, pepper, smoked paprika, and agave nectar. Mix well to combine, and season with more salt and pepper as needed and lemon juice (if using).

3 Chill, covered, for 1 hour or serve immediately, garnishing with sesame seeds and some more furikake. Store in an airtight container in the refrigerator for up to 3 days.

CRAB SALAD

¼ cup [60 g] Kewpie mayonnaise

2 Tbsp Dijon mustard

1 Tbsp soy sauce

1 Tbsp rice wine vinegar

½ Tbsp honey

1 tsp fresh lemon juice

1 tsp toasted sesame oil

½ tsp garlic powder

1 tsp smoked paprika

2 green onions, green and white parts finely chopped

1 lb [455 g] jumbo lump crabmeat, picked through and shell and cartilage removed

1 celery stalk, finely chopped

1 Persian or Kirby cucumber, seeded and finely chopped

1 carrot, cut into matchsticks

¼ cup [45 g] corn kernels

Kosher salt

Ground black pepper

Finely chopped fresh chives, for garnish

Roasted seaweed, crushed, for garnish

Toasted sesame seeds, for garnish

I didn't grow up with much crab in my house, even though it's one of Mom's favorites, for a very good reason: My dad is allergic to certain shellfish. For special occasions, though, Dad would buy live crabs to steam fresh for my mom. Those days were always a lot of fun, because us kids could mischievously play with the crabs, lifting them up with tongs in the big basket at the Korean market!

As for me, I'm allergic to raw fish and shellfish, so certain dishes, like ganjang gejang (soy sauce–marinated raw crab) are off-limits to me. But I wanted to make something special for my mom for a Mother's Day meal back when I was beginning my culinary career, so I turned to one of her favorite indulgences. There are some great (cooked) crab salads out there, including Japanese-style kani salad and American blue crab salad and now this recipe, made with a whole lot of love!

(cont.)

1 In a medium bowl, combine the mayonnaise, mustard, soy sauce, vinegar, honey, lemon juice, sesame oil, garlic powder, smoked paprika, and green onions.

2 To the bowl, add the crabmeat, celery, cucumber, carrot, and corn. Stir with a rubber spatula or large spoon until everything is coated. Season with salt and pepper.

3 Serve immediately, garnished with chopped chives, seaweed, and sesame seeds. Refrigerate leftovers in an airtight container for up to 3 days.

SMOKY GOCHUJANG CHICKEN SALAD SERVES 4 TO 5

2 Persian cucumbers or 1 English cucumber, seeded and thinly sliced

1 shallot, thinly sliced

1½ tsp kosher salt

1 tsp sugar

½ Tbsp white vinegar

1 tsp onion powder

½ tsp garlic powder

1 tsp smoked paprika

½ tsp hondashi

½ tsp ground black pepper

1 Tbsp Dijon mustard

1 Tbsp honey

1 Tbsp gochujang

½ Tbsp toasted sesame oil

½ Tbsp soy sauce

1 lb [455 g] shredded roasted chicken breast

Finely chopped green onion greens, for garnish

1 tsp toasted sesame seeds

Smoked sea salt, for garnish

Ready-made roast chicken has become increasingly available in the last few years, and with it, ideas for ways to use the leftover meat have proliferated.

There is one cold chicken salad dish that is usually seen at restaurants in the summertime: dak naengchae. It features shredded chicken in not mayo but a sesame dressing made with yeonggyeoja, a Korean mustard that packs a punch with its spiciness. I set out to make a similar spicy, mustardy chicken salad dish with leftover chicken and whatever I had in the house, and this is the result. Especially on warm nights when I don't want to turn on the stove, this is a go-to. In the summer, it goes on rotation in our home quite favorably. Feel free to add your favorite salad vegetables to it.

(cont.)

1   In a medium bowl, toss the cucumber with the shallot, salt, and sugar. Let sit for about 10 minutes to allow excess liquid to come out of the cucumber. Drain excess liquid.

2   Meanwhile, in a small bowl, combine the vinegar, onion powder, garlic powder, smoked paprika, hondashi, and pepper. Let sit for about 15 minutes to allow the hondashi to dissolve and the vinegar to infuse with all the flavors.

3   To the small bowl with the vinegar, add the mustard, honey, gochujang, sesame oil, and soy sauce. Stir together well to combine.

4   To the medium bowl with the cucumber, add the shredded chicken and toss well to combine, then add the mustard mixture, stirring until everything is well coated. Cover the bowl and refrigerate for about 20 minutes.

5   Garnish with green onion greens, the toasted sesame seeds, and a pinch or two of smoked sea salt, and serve. Store in an airtight container in the refrigerator for up to 3 days.

HOT

BANCHA

VEGETABLE ANCHOVY BROTH

8 cups [2 L] cold water

10 large dried anchovies, each about 3 in [7.5 cm] long

2 pieces dried kombu, each measuring 3 in [7.5 cm] square

1 carrot, cut into thirds

3 celery stalks, roughly chopped

2 oz [55 g] daikon radish, sliced

5 green onions

5 garlic cloves

8 oz [230 g] white or cremini mushrooms, sliced (optional)

1 tsp hondashi

After moving out of my parents' house, I had freedom to cook my own stuff, but I still wanted the best homey flavors every now and then—and this meant I needed to make a big batch of anchovy broth.

Anchovy broth is a staple in Korean cooking, and these days it's even more convenient to make with the advent of store-bought anchovy packets. (Opt for gukmulyong myeolchi—the larger anchovies that measure about 3 in [7.5 cm] long.) I take it up a notch by saving all my veggie scraps in a plastic bag in the freezer—even saving leftover mu (daikon radish) from Korean fried chicken orders—to make my own broth that has a traditional flavor but adds some new notes from my mix of vegetables. This broth makes a solid foundation to any soup, jjigae, or noodle dish, and serves up so much comfort.

When you're preparing this, remember to absolutely not scrub the white residue off the kombu. That's good built-in natural flavor right there!

1. In a 5 qt [4.7 L] pot, combine the water, anchovies, and kombu and let sit for about 30 minutes.

2. Add the carrot, celery, daikon, green onions, garlic, and mushrooms (if using), and bring the broth to a boil over medium-high heat.

3. Turn the heat to medium-low and add the hondashi, stirring to help it dissolve. Simmer for another 30 minutes (feel free to vent the lid if it starts to bubble over), or until your broth is fragrant and has a golden yellow hue.

4. Strain the broth into a heatproof jar (reserve the kombu, as you can cut it into pieces and have it as a snack). Use immediately, or store the broth in the refrigerator for up to 7 days. If you plan on freezing your broth, fill a storage container, leaving a 1½ in [4 cm] gap at the top to account for expansion when frozen, and freeze for up to 2 months.

GARLIC ANCHOVY OIL MAKES 1 CUP [240 ML]

1 Tbsp gochugaru

1½ cups [360 ml] grapeseed oil (or any neutral oil)

5 garlic cloves, thinly sliced

5 green onions, whites only, or 1 shallot, halved

1 bay leaf

1 oz [30 g] oil-packed anchovies, chopped

1 tsp honey

I'd grown up having only dried anchovies around my household, so I wasn't acquainted with having them any other way. However, that all changed when my husband and I took a trip to the Amalfi Coast in Italy. Let me tell you, he came back from that trip *invigorated* to have anchovies in all forms. Since then, we keep anchovies every which way—fresh, tinned, dried—in our home!

Anchovies are used in many cuisines; even a small number of these fish serve up big amounts of flavor, saltiness, and brininess. This recipe has been a staple in our household for the past decade for pan sauces, vegetable dressings, and in one case, even as a gift for our friend who loved it so much that they asked if I would write the recipe down so they could make it themselves. Similar to Korean chili oil, this infused oil is a pantry cousin to both fish sauce and chili oil. It's another oil to have on the table alongside rice and noodles, or even drizzled on pizza or your sandwiches!

To make this oil, I recommend using grapeseed or another oil with a high smoke point that can stand the heat. You can serve this sauce right away, or store it in a sealed jar in your fridge for up to a month to prolong its shelf life. If you find that the oil has solidified, spoon out your desired amount, and it will reliquefy quickly at room temperature.

However it fits in your home cooking, may it serve all delicious purposes!

(cont.)

1 To a heatproof glass measuring cup or small bowl, add the gochugaru. Set aside.

2 In a small pot or shallow saucepan over low heat, warm the grape-seed oil, garlic, green onion whites, bay leaf, and anchovies until the oil reaches about 200°F [95°C], or when you see that the garlic and green onions are browning and bubbling in the oil.

3 Turn off the heat. Remove the green onions, garlic, and bay leaf from the oil with tongs or a spider.

4 Pour the oil over the gochugaru (don't be stunned by the initial bubbling and sizzling! It will die down quickly). Let the oil steep for about 15 minutes.

5 Carefully add in the honey and stir until dissolved in the oil. Using a fine-mesh strainer, strain the oil into a sterilized glass storage jar. Use immediately, or let cool completely and store sealed in the refrigerator for up to 1 month.

MUSHROOM MISO SOUP SERVES 2 TO 4

2 green onions, green and white parts separated and chopped

3 garlic cloves, smashed

¼ cup [70 g] white miso paste

½ Tbsp hondashi

¼ cup [30 g] silken tofu, cubed

8 oz [230 g] baby bella mushrooms, sliced

2 oz [55 g] shiitake mushrooms, sliced into ½ in [13 mm] pieces

1 Tbsp wakame seaweed, rehydrated

note: *To best rehydrate wakame, place it in a bowl of warm water for about 15 minutes or until tender, and then squeeze out the excess water. This will also help get rid of any extra saltiness.*

Miso soup is, of course, Japanese in origin, but I've had it throughout my life alongside meals. This variation can take less time to make than your morning oatmeal and has plenty of health benefits too! If you've got more time and want to really get the best flavor, make your own dashi stock. However, because I'm usually pressed for time, I use hondashi (dried dashi powder) as a shortcut from the pantry (my Dad's trick!).

Whether served alongside gyeran mari (rolled omelette) or pickled vegetables, this soup goes well with any meal of the day. I keep it simple with shiitake and baby bella mushrooms or whatever is available at the market, but feel free to add some enoki mushrooms too!

A caution: Be sure to *never* let miso soup come to a boil—boil the water beforehand. Otherwise, you'll ruin the flavor of the miso and kill the probiotics along with it!

(cont.)

1 In a large pot over medium heat, combine 4 cups [960 ml] of water, the green onion whites, and the garlic. Bring the water to a boil, then turn the heat to low and bring to a simmer.

2 Meanwhile, in a small bowl, combine the miso paste and a small amount of hot water from the pot, stirring it with chopsticks or a fork until the miso paste loosens to a smooth liquid and has no lumps. Add this to the simmering (not boiling!) broth along with the hondashi, and stir.

3 Add the tofu, both mushrooms, and wakame. Cover and let the soup simmer for about 3 minutes, or until the mushrooms are cooked to your liking.

4 Ladle the soup into bowls, garnishing with the green onion greens. Serve hot. Once cooled, store leftovers in an airtight container in the refrigerator for up to 4 days or in the freezer for up to 3 months.

TOMATO POTATO MISO SOUP SERVES 4 TO 5

Cooking oil

2 green onions, green and white parts separated and finely chopped

2 garlic cloves, smashed

2 red potatoes, peeled and chopped into 1 in [2.5 cm] pieces

14.5 oz [410 g] can crushed San Marzano tomatoes

½ Tbsp hondashi

¼ cup [70 g] white miso paste

½ cup [120 ml] milk

1 Tbsp unsalted butter

This is a hearty, go-to soup in all seasons. It's light enough for summer if chilled, but incredibly comforting when served hot in cold weather. There's a layer of creaminess to it from the potato starch, saltiness and added flavor from the miso and hondashi, and a little extra comfort from a touch of butter and milk.

1. Set a 5 qt [4.7 L] pot over medium heat and lightly coat the bottom of the pot with oil. Allow the oil to heat for about 1 minute. Add the green onion whites, garlic, and potatoes and cook, stirring, until the green onions and garlic have softened and turned golden brown.

2. Add the crushed tomatoes and cook, stirring, for 2 minutes.

3. Add 4 cups [960 ml] of water and stir together until fully combined. Allow the broth to come to a boil, and then turn the heat to low to let it simmer for 25 to 30 minutes, until the potatoes are fork-tender.

4. Add the hondashi and stir until it dissolves.

5. In a cup or small bowl, combine the miso paste and a small amount of hot liquid from the pot, stirring with chopsticks or a fork until the miso paste loosens to a smooth liquid with no lumps. Add the miso liquid to the simmering liquid and stir to combine.

6. Remove the pot from the heat and add the milk and butter. Stir until the butter has melted. Allow the soup to cool for about 20 minutes.

7. With an immersion blender, blend the soup until completely smooth. Garnish with green onion greens and serve immediately. Once cooled, store leftovers in an airtight container in the refrigerator for up to 4 days or freeze for up to 1 month.

ASPARAGUS WITH MAPLE DOENJANG DIPPING SAUCE SERVES 4

2 Tbsp maple syrup

1 Tbsp doenjang

2 tsp soy sauce

1 tsp toasted sesame oil

½ tsp toasted sesame seeds

¼ tsp ground black pepper

Kosher salt

1 lb [455 g] cooked asparagus

My parents like to be inventive with their sauces and dressings for vegetables. I'm happy to be the beneficiary of their "simple suppers"—which is what they call their vegetable-based meals with creative sauces—and whatever other surprises come out of their pantry. In this case, my dad created this vegetable dipping sauce one summer, and it couldn't be simpler to throw together. All you need is some asparagus, cooked however you prefer it. Then, dip away!

1   In a small bowl, combine the maple syrup, doenjang, soy sauce, sesame oil, sesame seeds, and pepper. Whisk with a fork until no lumps remain.

2   Season with salt to taste, and serve with the asparagus.

GIM GYERAN MARI (ROLLED OMELETTE WITH SEAWEED) SERVES 2 TO 3

3 eggs

½ Tbsp toasted sesame oil

Kosher salt

Ground black pepper

Cooking oil

1 sheet roasted seaweed

Toasted sesame seeds, for garnish

This comfort food looks as good as it tastes. Lots of folks will make their gyeran mari with added vegetables or ham, but this version is my favorite and conveniently involves no additional prep. My dad makes it along with special-occasion sashimi (Japanese sliced raw fish) and sushi meals for my mom, and for early morning breakfasts before watching the World Cup. Whether served in your dosirak (Korean packaged lunchbox), or eaten as your daily protein, it's absolutely delicious, and beautiful when sliced up too!

(cont.)

1   In a medium bowl, beat the eggs with the sesame oil and a generous seasoning of salt and pepper.

2   Set a medium nonstick frying pan over medium-low heat and lightly coat the bottom of the pan with cooking oil. Allow the oil to heat for 1 to 2 minutes.

3   When the oil is hot, pour in about half of the beaten eggs, swirling the pan until the entire bottom of the pan is covered. Turn the heat down to low and let the egg cook for a little less than 1 minute; when the egg is set but the surface is still wet, carefully lay the roasted seaweed sheet on top of the egg.

4   Pour the remaining beaten egg over the seaweed and tilt the pan to spread the egg mixture evenly across the top.

5   When the egg surface has just set but is still a bit runny, with the aid of a spatula, lift one end of the egg and fold it over about 1½ in [4 cm]. Repeat with more folds until you've created a nice, rolled egg log in the pan!

6   Transfer the log to a cutting board, and let it cool for about a minute before slicing the log into 1 in [2.5 cm] pieces.

7   Garnish with sesame seeds and season with a few pinches each of salt and pepper, and serve. Store any leftovers in an airtight container in the fridge for up to 3 days. Can be eaten hot or cold!

CHEESY CORN SERVES 4 TO 6

Cooking oil

2 cups [345 g] canned or frozen corn

3 green onions, white and green parts separated and chopped

1 garlic clove, minced, or ½ tsp garlic powder

Kosher salt

Ground black pepper

½ cup [40 g] shredded extra-sharp Cheddar cheese

2 Tbsp mascarpone cheese

2 Tbsp mayonnaise

½ tsp sugar

½ tsp smoked paprika

¼ tsp mustard powder

1 cup [80 g] shredded part-skim mozzarella cheese

¼ cup [25 g] Cotija or pecorino cheese

Cheesy corn has become a very popular gastropub dish in Korea, and what's not to love about it? Corn plus a delightful cheese pull? Goes perfect with a few drinks and chips, but small portions of it can go well with your KBBQ spread. This is the recipe I've made and shared with friends, and it goes *fast*.

There are all sorts of personal preferences at play in this recipe: To save time chopping, I skip bell peppers and just call for garlic and smoked paprika for flavor. I prefer using fresh corn for a bit more bite and lots of natural sweetness, but if you'd like to spare yourself the prep time, canned or frozen works too. Regular mayo is great, but if you have Kewpie mayo, it's even better! I find it easiest to prepare this in a cast-iron skillet so I only have to clean one dish, but if you have a trusty frying pan and glass baking dish, it'll get the job done too!

(cont.)

1   Preheat the oven to 400°F [200°C].

2   Set a cast-iron skillet over medium heat and lightly coat the bottom of the pan with cooking oil. Allow the oil to heat for about 1 minute. Add the corn, green onion whites, garlic, and a pinch of salt and pepper and cook, stirring, until the green onions are softened and golden brown. Remove the skillet from the heat and let cool for about 15 minutes.

3   Add the Cheddar, mascarpone, mayonnaise, sugar, smoked paprika, mustard powder, 1 tsp salt, and ½ tsp pepper, and stir well to combine.

4   Top with the mozzarella and carefully transfer the skillet to the oven. Bake for 15 to 20 minutes, until the cheese is melted and bubbly. If you like it without a crispy top, remove from the oven and let the skillet cool for about 10 minutes. If you want a crispy cheese top, set the skillet under the broiler for 5 minutes, then remove and let the skillet cool for about 10 minutes.

5   Garnish with Cotija and chopped green onion greens, and serve up hot! Store any leftovers in an airtight container in the refrigerator for up to 4 days.

SWEET & SAVORY GRILLED KIMCHEESE ^{SERVES 1}

1 Tbsp unsalted butter, plus more as needed

2 slices sandwich bread

1 Tbsp goat cheese

1 tsp fig jam

¼ cup [40 g] napa cabbage kimchi, such as Mom & Dad's Kimchi (page 28), finely chopped

¼ cup [20 g] shredded extra-sharp Cheddar cheese

This recipe highlights the commonalities between kimchi and cheese. They're both fermented and delicious; more than that, they're both ingredients that can fit into almost any meal. Many chefs have their own great recipes for kimchi cheese sandwiches: Joanne Molinaro, the Korean Vegan; J. Kenji López-Alt; and my dear friend Eric Kim all have their versions. However, this is my favorite combination for a kimchi grilled cheese, with a little added sweetness from fig jam to go with the beloved funkiness.

(cont.)

1   Set a large frying pan or skillet over medium-low heat, and melt the butter, swirling to coat the bottom of the pan.

2   Place both slices of bread in the pan side by side and allow them to toast on one side for about 1 minute, then transfer them to a plate, toasted side up. Turn off the heat under the pan for now.

3   On the toasted side of one slice of bread, carefully spread the goat cheese. Spoon on and spread the fig jam on top of the goat cheese using the back of the spoon. Place the kimchi on top in an even layer. Lastly, pile the Cheddar on top of the kimchi, and place the other bread slice, toasted-side down, on top of the Cheddar (its warmth will help it stick to the cheese).

4   Turn the heat under the frying pan to medium-low and melt more butter if the pan is dry. Place the sandwich into the pan, lightly pressing on the surface with the back of a spatula, and cook for 2 to 3 minutes, or until the bottom of the bread is toasted. You might hear some cheese sizzling on the pan. Carefully flip the sandwich over, pressing lightly again to toast the other side, another 1 to 2 minutes, depending how toasty you'd like your bread to be.

5   Transfer the sandwich to a plate and allow it to cool for about 1 minute before cutting in half and serving hot.

BIBIMBAP SERVES 4

GOCHUJANG SAUCE

¼ cup [60 ml] toasted sesame oil

2 Tbsp gochujang

2 Tbsp rice wine vinegar

1 Tbsp honey

1 garlic clove, minced

2 tsp toasted sesame seeds

BIBIMBAP

1 lb [455 g] thinly sliced rib eye

1 Tbsp soy sauce

1 Tbsp toasted sesame oil

1 tsp sugar

1 tsp ground black pepper

Cooking oil

2 green onions, white and green parts separated and chopped

1 carrot, cut into matchsticks

Kosher salt

1 lb [455 g] shiitake or button mushrooms, sliced

4 cups [720 g] steamed short-grain white sushi rice, still hot

2 Persian or Kirby cucumbers, cut into matchsticks

Shigeumchi Namul (page 48)

Kongnamul Muchim (page 50)

Gosari Namul (page 61)

4 eggs

I said before that banchan finds a home in Kimbap (page 137), but it also finds wide-open space to run in a bowl of bibimbap! Whether served as dolsot bibimbap, sizzling in a hot earthenware bowl, or in a large ceramic bowl out of my parents' cabinet, bibimbap always provides a good hefty meal. Mix it with this quick gochujang sauce, and happy eating!

MAKE THE SAUCE:

1   In a small bowl, combine the sesame oil, gochujang, vinegar, honey, garlic, and sesame seeds, mixing well with a fork. Set aside.

(cont.)

MAKE THE BIBIMBAP:

1. In a bowl, combine the rib eye with the soy sauce, sesame oil, sugar, and pepper, tossing until the rib eye is fully coated. Cover and set aside in the refrigerator to marinate for at least 30 minutes.

2. In a medium skillet over medium-high heat, cook the rib eye for 3 to 5 minutes, or until the meat is cooked through but still tender. Remove from the heat and transfer to a plate. Set aside.

3. Drain any liquid from the pan, wipe out the pan, set it over medium heat, and lightly coat the bottom of the pan with cooking oil. Allow the oil to heat for about 1 minute. Add half of the green onion whites and cook for about 2 minutes, or until golden brown. Add the carrot, season with a pinch of salt, and cook for about 2 minutes. Transfer the carrot, green onion whites, and half of the green onion greens to a plate or bowl, and set aside.

4. Return the pan to medium heat and add a bit more cooking oil to the pan. Add the rest of the green onion whites and cook for 2 minutes, or until translucent and golden brown. Add the mushrooms, season them with a pinch of salt, and cook for about 5 minutes, or until the mushrooms are tender (not soggy!). Transfer the mushrooms and green onion to a plate or bowl, add the remaining green onion greens to the plate, and set aside.

5. Divide the hot cooked rice among four serving bowls. (Larger serving bowls are helpful for mixing it up.) On top of the rice, make piles of the rib eye, carrot, mushrooms, cucumbers, shigeumchi namul, kongnamul nuchim, and gosari namul.

6. Set a large skillet over medium heat and lightly coat the bottom of the pan with cooking oil. Fry the eggs on one side for 3 minutes or until the whites set to make sunny-side up eggs. (I like them over-easy for bibimbap too—a runny yolk is the important part.) Set a fried egg on top of each bowl of rice.

7. Serve with the sauce on the side. Each person can add sauce to their liking, then mix it all up before eating. If you have leftovers, store in an airtight container in the refrigerator for just 24 hours; after that the rice will get hard and won't be as good.

SPRING GREENS NAMUL QUICHE ^{SERVES 8}

Olive oil

1 shallot, chopped

2 green onions, green and white parts separated and finely chopped

8 oz [230 g] asparagus, cut into 1 in [2.5 cm] pieces

½ cup [170 g] frozen baby peas

6 eggs

1½ cups [360 ml] heavy cream

¼ cup [60 ml] 2% Greek yogurt

1 tsp kosher salt

½ tsp dried thyme

½ tsp ground black pepper

¼ cup [20 g] shredded Cheddar cheese

1 frozen shortbread pie shell, not defrosted

½ cup [120 g] Shigeumchi Namul (page 48)

I made this quiche for one of my clients a few years ago, and she told me she was bewildered at how she'd missed out on enjoying vegetables for so long! It was one of the best compliments I've ever received, but of course, when those vegetables are in a buttery crust, what's not to love?

In the event that you have some leftover namul (pages 46 to 63) in your fridge, here is another dish those fresh veg can find their way into. My favorite namul to add to this recipe is Shigeumchi Namul (page 48), and since it is already seasoned, it provides another depth of flavor to your spring greens quiche! I call for Cheddar cheese in this recipe, but other cheeses can work just as well: fontina, pepper jack, paneer, or even a nice Roquefort. Serve hot, eat your leftovers cold.

(cont.)

1 Preheat the oven to 350°F [180°C].

2 Set a medium skillet over medium heat and lightly coat the bottom of the pan with olive oil. Allow the oil to heat for about 1 minute. Add the chopped shallot, green onion whites, and asparagus and cook for 3 minutes, until the asparagus is slightly tender on the outside (but not cooked all the way through).

3 Add the peas and cook for another minute. Transfer the mixture to a bowl or plate and set aside.

4 In a large bowl, whisk together the eggs, cream, yogurt, green onion greens, salt, thyme, and pepper. Stir in the cheese.

5 Remove the pie shell from the freezer. Spread out the shigeumchi, asparagus, peas, and green onion whites on the bottom of the crust. Pour the egg mixture over the vegetables.

6 Bake the quiche for 40 to 45 minutes, or until the quiche is set with a slight wobble and the crust is golden brown.

7 Let the quiche cool and set for 20 minutes before serving. Store leftover quiche in an airtight container in the refrigerator for up to 3 days.

"HOT HONEY" CRISPY TOFU

14 oz [400 g] block firm tofu

¼ cup [60 ml] agave nectar

2 Tbsp gochujang

1 Tbsp apple cider vinegar

½ tsp liquid smoke

¼ cup [40 g] potato starch or cornstarch

1 tsp smoked paprika

1 tsp onion powder

1 tsp kosher salt

½ tsp garlic powder

½ tsp ground black pepper

¼ tsp mustard powder

¼ tsp cayenne pepper

Cooking oil

Toasted sesame seeds, for garnish

Chopped green onion greens, for garnish

I once babysat for a family whose young children were big fans of crispy tofu, so I cooked it at least two or three times a week. When I began my chef career, I decided to cook this for clients who were looking for plant-based comfort dishes, and this quickly became their most-requested side dish alongside a full meal!

(cont.)

1   Drain the tofu, wrap the block in paper towels or a clean dish towel, and place on a plate. Set a heavy, flat object (a frying pan or cast-iron skillet works well) on top and leave it for about 30 minutes to press the liquid out.

2   Meanwhile, make the "hot honey." In a small bowl, combine the agave nectar, gochujang, vinegar, and liquid smoke. Set aside.

3   Slice the pressed tofu into ½ in [13 mm] slices, and set to rest on a plate lined with fresh paper towels.

4   On a separate plate, gently whisk together the potato starch, smoked paprika, onion powder, salt, garlic powder, black pepper, mustard powder, and cayenne.

5   Gently dredge the tofu slices in the seasoned starch.

6   Set a large skillet over medium heat and lightly coat the bottom of the pan with cooking oil. Allow the oil to heat for about 1 minute or until the oil is shimmering. Fry the tofu in batches, cooking for 2 to 3 minutes on each side, or until both sides are crispy and golden-brown. Transfer the slices to a plate lined with paper towels as they are ready. Repeat until all the tofu is fried.

7   Transfer the tofu to a serving plate and drizzle the "hot honey" all over. Garnish with sesame seeds and green onion greens. Serve hot. Though it will lose its crispiness when refrigerated, leftover tofu can be stored in an airtight container in the fridge for up to 4 days. If you want to attempt to revive some crispiness, reheat in a lightly oiled pan over medium heat on both sides.

KIMCHI BOKKEUMBAP (KIMCHI FRIED RICE) SERVES 2 TO 3

Cooking oil

1 cup [150 g] aged napa cabbage kimchi, such as Mom & Dad's Kimchi (page 28), chopped

2 cups [360 g] day-old steamed short-grain white sushi rice

2 Tbsp toasted sesame oil

1 Tbsp soy sauce

3 eggs

1 green onion, green and white parts chopped

Roasted seaweed, thinly sliced, for garnish

When my dad asked me once what I'd like him to cook for my birthday, I told him simply: "Your kalbi, and kimchi bokkeumbap."

There are some dishes in this world that will make your mouth water just thinking about them, and kimchi bokkeumbap is one of them for me. It is undoubtedly one of my best-loved comfort foods. It never tastes the same to me at restaurants—this is home cooking at its best. Enjoy the aromas while cooking it, top it all off with a fried egg, and savor every bite!

1   Set a large nonstick frying pan over medium heat and lightly coat the bottom of the pan with cooking oil. Allow the oil to heat for about 1 minute. Add the kimchi and sauté, stirring with a wooden spoon for 5 to 7 minutes, or until the cabbage is caramelized on some of the edges.

2   Add the rice, sesame oil, and soy sauce, and stir to combine. If you want the rice to have a crisp texture, let the rice sit, undisturbed, for 1 minute. Transfer the mixture to serving bowls.

3   Wipe the pan clean, or place a separate nonstick frying pan over medium heat and lightly coat the bottom with cooking oil. Heat the oil for 1 minute, then add the eggs and cook until the egg whites have set and are no longer runny and clear.

4   Top each serving of kimchi rice with a fried egg, and garnish with green onion and seaweed.

PORK BELLY & VEGETABLE BOKKEUM SERVES 2 TO 4

1½ Tbsp soy sauce

1 Tbsp toasted sesame oil

½ Tbsp sugar

2 tsp ground black pepper

1 tsp gochugaru

8 oz [230 g] thick-cut pork belly, cut into ½ in [13 mm] pieces

Cooking oil

3 green onions, green and white parts separated and finely chopped

2 garlic cloves, minced

1 cup [98 g] snow peas

1 carrot, cut into matchsticks or thinly sliced

Bokkeum is a classic quick stir-fry with sweet and savory flavor. This bokkeum is spicy thanks to the black pepper and gochugaru, so I like to serve it along with a bowl of rice and some soup. But if you want to make a tasty spicy sauce to go with this, by all means, go for it! A bit of gochujang, sesame oil, mirin, and soy sauce whisked together would be delicious.

1   In a small bowl, combine the soy sauce, sesame oil, sugar, pepper, and gochugaru. Mix well until the sugar dissolves. Set aside.

2   In a large nonstick skillet over medium heat, cook the pork belly (no need for oil, since the pork belly is plenty fatty). Cook, lightly tossing, for about 3 minutes, until all pieces are browned and just cooked through. Remove from the pan and set aside on a plate.

3   Strain the fat in the pan into a heatproof bowl for later use or disposal, wipe the pan clean with a paper towel, then return the pan to medium heat. Lightly coat the bottom of the pan with cooking oil. Allow the oil to heat for about 1 minute. Add the green onion whites, garlic, snow peas, and carrot. Toss and cook for 2 minutes, or until the green onion and garlic are golden brown.

4   Turn the heat to medium-low and return the pork belly to the pan, stirring to combine. Pour the sauce over and let cook, stirring, for 2 minutes, or until the vegetables are tender and the sauce is well incorporated.

5   Garnish with the green onion greens and serve hot! Store any leftovers in an airtight container in the refrigerator for up to 4 days.

KIMCHI MAC & CHEESE SERVES 6 TO 8

1 lb [455 g] cavatappi or any tube pasta

6 Tbsp [170 g] unsalted butter

4 oz [115 g] spicy napa cabbage kimchi, such as Mom & Dad's Kimchi (page 28), chopped into 1 in [2.5 cm] pieces

2 Tbsp all-purpose flour

2 cups [480 ml] whole milk

1 tsp kosher salt

½ tsp ground white pepper

¼ tsp mustard powder

¼ tsp smoked paprika

1 lb [455 g] extra-sharp Cheddar cheese, grated

8 oz [230 g] Gruyère cheese, grated

¼ cup [20 g] grated pecorino cheese

¼ cup [60 ml] 2% Greek yogurt (optional)

Crumbled cooked bacon, for garnish (optional)

Chopped green onions, for garnish (optional)

I thought there was no dish more crowd-pleasing than mac and cheese, until I served this kimchi mac at an event and it emptied faster than I could fill it back up. Whenever I bring this to family, friend, and client events, everyone is always excited to see it—which, of course, is the happiest reaction a chef could ever receive.

This celebration of fermented food is a fantastic dish you will truly crave. I find that the trick is sautéing the kimchi in butter. Since kimchi is acidic from the pickling and has lots of liquid from the napa cabbage, sautéing it will help lower the water content and concentrate the natural flavors and oils. It also creates an incredible mornay sauce (a béchamel sauce with cheese) that won't separate itself from the milk solids. Best of all, kimchi packs such an incredible punch of flavor; it's guaranteed to enhance your already delicious mac.

Good food may take time (as both the kimchi and cheese can personally attest to), but this is a fun one to make. I enjoy every second of making this as much as I do eating it!

(cont.)

1   Cook the pasta according to the package instructions until al dente. Before straining the pasta, carefully measure and reserve 5 Tbsp [75 ml] of the pasta water. Drain the pasta completely and set aside.

2   In a 5 qt [4.7 L] pot over medium-high heat, melt the butter, tilting the pot to coat the bottom. Let it heat for about 1 minute. Add the chopped kimchi and sauté for 5 to 7 minutes, until the cabbage has softened and the liquid has reduced by about half.

3   Add the flour, whisking it with the kimchi until completely combined to create a roux.

4   Gradually add the milk, whisking constantly. Turn the heat to low and continue whisking, occasionally gently scraping up the sticky bits at the bottom of the pot with the whisk.

5   Add the salt, white pepper, mustard powder, and smoked paprika, and continue whisking for about 3 minutes, or until the sauce thickens.

6   Gradually add the Cheddar, Gruyère, and pecorino cheeses and stir with a wooden spoon until they all have melted into the sauce and the texture is smooth.

7   Gradually fold the cooked pasta into the sauce until combined. Add the reserved pasta water to ensure the pasta bonds with the kimchi sauce and to thin out the sauce's consistency.

8   Remove from the heat and mix in the yogurt (if using; it adds a bit of tanginess). Garnish with bacon crumbles (if using), and green onions (if using). Serve it up hot. Store any leftovers in an airtight container in the refrigerator for up to 5 days. To reheat in the micro-wave, place the kimchi mac in a microwave-safe bowl and heat on high for 1 minute. To reheat on the stove, place the kimchi mac in a pot or skillet with a generous splash of milk over medium-low heat, breaking it up and stirring with a wooden spoon. It tastes even better the next day!

PA MUCHIM PIZZA SERVES 4 TO 5

WHITE SAUCE

¼ cup [55 g] unsalted butter

¼ cup [35 g] all-purpose flour

2 cups [480 ml] 2% milk

¼ cup [22 g] grated Parmesan cheese

1 tsp kosher salt

½ tsp ground black pepper

½ tsp onion powder

¼ tsp garlic powder

PIZZA

All-purpose flour, for sprinkling

10 oz [285 g] ball pizza dough

1½ cups [170 g] shredded low-moisture mozzarella cheese

1 cup [100 g] Pa Muchim (page 56), plus more for garnish

4 oz [115 g] smoked ham, thinly sliced

Gochugaru, for garnish (optional)

Toasted sesame seeds, for garnish (optional)

I am certainly not the only person out there who has put muchim on pizza. However, if you're going to do it, I hope you choose pa muchim—and may it make you very happy to do so!

In the beginning of the pandemic, I was ALL about making pizza, whipping up countless batches of Jim Lahey's no-knead pizza dough and practicing my stretching, while heating up our tiny apartment with our tiny oven. I made do with whatever toppings I could get my hands on, for there were only limited supplies available in stores. Pa muchim was a winner. Its subtle sweet, tangy, and spicy qualities made for a damn good pizza topping.

Feel free to make this with or without ham, but definitely try it with some sesame seeds or gochugaru at the end for a little kick. If you have fresh buffalo mozzarella, go for it and add as much cheese as you want! You could also add some fresh arugula or a drizzle of Garlic Anchovy Oil (page 160); spice it up however you like! No matter what, this is my definition of happy food.

(cont.)

MAKE THE WHITE SAUCE:

1 Set a small saucepan over medium-low and melt the butter.

2 Add the flour and whisk until the mixture is smooth, to create a roux.

3 Gradually add the milk and continue whisking until thickened.

4 Add the Parmesan, salt, pepper, onion powder, and garlic powder. Stir until fully combined. Set the sauce aside to cool.

MAKE THE PIZZA:

1 Preheat oven to 500°F [260°C].

2 Spread out a 20 by 15 in [51 by 38 cm] piece of aluminum foil and sprinkle flour over the surface. Gently stretch the dough with your fingers until it measures 10 to 12 in [25 to 30.5 cm] in diameter or so—don't worry if it's not perfectly round! Transfer the dough, on the foil, to a 12 by 17 in [30.5 by 43 cm] baking sheet.

3 Ladle an even layer of the white sauce on the dough, leaving a 1 in [2.5 cm] border.

4 Sprinkle the mozzarella over the sauce in an even layer, then distribute the pa muchim and ham over the top.

5 Bake the pizza for about 20 minutes, or until the crust is browned and crispy and the mozzarella is melted and bubbly.

6 Remove from the oven and allow the pizza to cool for 15 minutes before garnishing with gochugaru (if using) and sesame seeds (if using). Slice and serve hot.

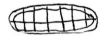

ACKNOWLEDGMENTS

First and foremost, thank you to my family, which spans far and wide and includes many people who have shared stories and delicious food over many lifetimes. It took a very long time to finally get even a portion of this family's shenanigans documented on paper, but I'm glad to have served the cause! Though I'll probably never truly know everyone's secrets to making food, I'm happy that every conversation about them has led to this moment. Thanks for enriching my Korean American life. Your excitement and support are immensely valued, and every bit of encouragement has helped me more than you all know.

To my Mom and Dr. Dad, Kathy, Pat, Jen, Madeleine and Mila, the Keans and Harveys, Kay and Harold Cadena, and everyone in the many limbs of this family tree (and, my goodness, there are a lot of branches to this tree!).

My art team was a phenomenal group of some of the hardest working and best women in the biz. Huge, immense thanks to my photographer, Ghazalle Badiozamani, and Grace Puffer for her assistance. Your strength and compassion got me through all of it, and the visuals are beautiful because of you. I'm incredibly grateful for the magical place that is Blue Salt Studios in New York City, and especially thankful that this was the place we were able to have such a wonderful collaboration over just a few days!

Cheers to the prop team that is Nicole Louie and Colin Favre. I lift a glass especially to Nicole for being a total queen multitasker, pumping for your baby while still selecting and sorting all those beautiful props!

To my food stylist team of Julia Choi-Rodriguez and the incredible Erica Santiago—the well of gratitude to you both runs deep. Julia, I told you one day we'd do a book together, and God heard the words. Years later, here we are! Thank you both for giving the best chef mama energy on set, which I was fantastically lucky just to witness.

Toby Klinger, thank you for always making this girl feel beautiful!

To the members of our squad of helping hands who also came through when we needed them! This includes dear friends John Eckels and Chris Nelson, and also the awesome husbands of the art team on this shoot for jumping in to help: Roger, Max, and, of course, Eric!

To my literary agent, Lindsey Smith—thank you for being with me on this ride! To quote one of your favorites, Taylor Swift: "Once upon a time, the planets and the fates and all the stars aligned." I still remember that very first conversation we had and how you helped me navigate this entire process. I feel very lucky to have shared as many laughs as we have. Thank you for being with me whichever way and however you've been able!

To the team at Chronicle Books—Jessica Ling, Rachel Harrell, Tera Killip, and Steve Kim—thank you for putting together this cookbook and all your efforts to help make it what it ultimately became.

However, the biggest hugs amongst the Chronicle team go to my editor, Claire Gilhuly. I thank you for meeting me with kindness, patience, and belief that this was a book we could best create together. We did it!

My first career in education offered me the opportunity to meet and teach some of the most memorable kids and families, and I will forever be indebted to the community from that part of my life. Believe it or not, I remember you all! A special thanks to my fifth grade students in 2014 who told me as we were learning about "hopes and dreams" that creating food was part of my hopes and dreams. I hope you all embark on the greatest adventures and fulfill every hope and dream you have too. Keep striving for the stars. I'm cheering you on!

Thank you also to everyone I crossed paths with in my teaching career and in my own education who impacted my life for the better and supported me during this current professional chapter. You're always in my heart.

To give a loving shout-out to every encouraging friend would be a very long list, but I promise you all that I'll never take for granted how incredibly blessed and privileged I am to have such a circle of friends. Whether you were testing recipes in your kitchens or tasting them at small get-togethers, or even just offering a lifeline when things got very tough: thank you. No uplifting word or heartening gesture was taken lightly on this journey.

I extend an extra special thanks for the advice and camaraderie offered in this process by many in this AANHPI community, but certainly not limited to: Jasmine Cho, Eric Kim, Lucy Yu, Aram Kim, Carol Yu, Abi Balingit, Hannah Bae, Maangchi, Emi Boscamp, Cathy Erway, Sohui Kim, Jaeki Cho, Joanne Molinaro, Christen Smith, and Sung Mun Choi.

Helen Cho, you are unstoppable and amazing. Thank you so much for your kind words, and for always working and pressing for the better. You are appreciated far more than you know.

To my husband, Eric Cadena: Words can't say what love can do. You once said I never need to tell you "thank you." So, I won't! However, I'll just proclaim here in print that you are, indeed, one of the coolest and best people on the planet. I'm forever your biggest fan.

It's been said before, but I'll say it again: There's not one way to be Korean, let alone Korean American. For all those continuing to learn, love, and be who you are, this book is especially for you. Thank you for being you, and keep shining your light brightly.

INDEX

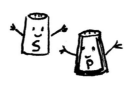